ENDING 'BIG SIS'

(The Special Interest State)

and Renewing
the American Republic

James V. DeLong

Cover design by David Strong

ISBN: 147000626X
ISBN 13: 9781470006266

Library of Congress Control Number: 2012901977
CreateSpace, North Charleston, SC

Dedication

To all citizen activists, for reviving real hope for real change

and

To Dianne, for demonstrating the American entrepreneurial spirit

Contents

Note on Style and References

Punctuation

This essay places punctuation marks outside of quotation marks, unless the punctuation mark is part of the quotation. The U.S. practice of putting these marks within the quotation produces needless ambiguity.

The essay also uses the Oxford comma, which places a comma after the second in a series of three, as in "black, white, and yellow". This, too, avoids unnecessary ambiguity.

Endnotes

The essay does not contain footnotes, as many readers find them distracting. An endnotes section identifies sources of quotations and particular statements, albeit sparingly. This book is appearing simultaneously in printed and e-book formats, and page numbers in e-books are variable. Hence, the endnotes are not pegged to page numbers in the text. To orient the reader, each note is introduced by a few words to establish its context. The titles of the sections and subsections of the book are also repeated in the endnotes, except when a particular subdivision contains no notes.

References

A references section lists the major sources used. It is divided into five categories:

> Books;
> Major Articles, Studies, and Monographs;
> Government Sources;
> News Clips, Weblogs, and Miscellaneous; and
> Legal Decisions.

Web links are not included, but can be found on the supporting website: www.specialintereststate.org.

Chapter One

Introduction to Big SIS

"A Republic, if you can keep it"

Benjamin Franklin had a gift for the quotable, and one of his best-known aphorisms came as he left the Constitutional Convention in 1787. "Well, Doctor," he was asked, "What have we got—a Republic or a Monarchy?" He answered, "A Republic, if you can keep it."

The Founders of the nation knew that a republican form of government was indeed hard to keep, and they agonized over its vulnerabilities. High on their list was the fear that particular groups might capture the government and turn its power to their own benefit.

The Founders called such a group a "faction", defined by Madison as "a number of citizens, whether amounting to a majority or a minority of the whole, who are united and actuated by some common impulse of passion, or of interest, adversed to the rights of other citizens, or to the permanent and aggregate interests of the community."

They were aware that the existence of factions cannot be prevented, and their goal was to establish a structure of government that would control their corrosive effects. Like architects analyzing the lines of force necessary to prevent the collapse of a building, the Founders focused on making the forces of factional passion neutralize each other, thus keeping the republic standing. The U.S. Constitution reflects this model of offsetting forces, as it divides sovereignty between state and federal governments and then further divides the federal powers among mutually wary branches.

The thesis of this book is simple. It is that U.S. politics has gone astray by losing this fundamental insight of the Founders. Rather than maintain a government designed to prevent and control the power of faction, we have allowed a wide variety of factions to capture parts of the government and then use the government's powers to spend, to tax, to legislate, and to regulate for their own purposes.

The term "factions" is not commonly used now, but "special interests" is a reasonable synonym. Thus, we can call our current political structure "Big SIS", which is short for "the Special Interest State".

Some other terms describing factions are also useful for analysis and discussion. Economist Mancur Olson, who wrote several indispensable books on interest groups and government, called them "distributional coalitions". "Clients" is a good term, too, especially when applied to the beneficiaries of a particular government program, because it captures the interdependence of private groups and government administrators. All of these terms are used in this essay.

"A dreadful image of a spreading rot"

To say we have "allowed" capture is too weak. Our current politics do not just *allow* it. We *celebrate* Big SIS. Our educated elites, in particular, regard the ability of factions to hijack governmental power for private benefit as an unavoidable characteristic of our system, perhaps even a basic right. Control by special interests is not an evil to be resisted; it is a feature rather than a bug.

Even worse, we have embraced a virulent form of Big SIS called "systemic corruption". In this model, political operators create economic advantages for special interests and then demand that part of the profits be fed back into the political system, where they are used to enhance the power of the operators. For example, a university might benefit from a congressional earmark, and its trustees might then contribute to the reelection campaign of the earmarker, or its faculty might help write his speeches. An energy company might receive federal loan guarantees, with the *quid pro quo* of supporting a president's next campaign. A pharmaceutical trade association might receive special benefits in a health care bill in exchange for funding a PR campaign in support of the legislation.

Our eighteenth– and nineteenth-century ancestors would be horrified at what we have wrought, because they knew that systemic corruption is fatal to republican government. In the 1800s, says historian Lance Banning: "['Corruption'] most often brought to mind a...dreadful image of a spreading rot. A frequent metaphor compared corruption to organic cancer, eating at the vitals of the body politic."

They were right, and many modern examples vindicate their foresight.

For 2010, the Taxpayers for Common Sense database lists almost 12,000 congressional appropriations earmarks worth $39 billion. Anyone who knows the game is aware that a portion of earmarks get laundered back into campaign contributions, or repaid by profitable inside information, or other benefits for representatives and their staffs.

"Cash for Clunkers" destroyed 750,000 drivable cars, which raised the used car prices paid by the poorest segment of the population for the benefit of newly government-subsidized auto companies and their unions. Few asked the question posed by columnist Jeff Jacoby: "Poorer drivers will be penalized to subsidize new cars for wealthier drivers. Isn't that immoral?"

In November 2011, eighty-five Senators opposed cutting a billion dollars from the Rural Development Agency, described by Senator Jim DeMint as a notorious pork barrel that "has used taxpayer money to make profligate loans to casinos, beach resorts, and water parks."

Public employee unions bargain with politicians; then they collect dues, which are recycled back into contributions to the politicians who are supposed to be bargaining on behalf of the public. The unions also have a great capacity to put boots on the ground to turn out the vote, a crucial factor in most down-ballot elections.

A personal experience: In the 1960s, while working on urban mass-transit issues for the Department of Housing and Urban Development, I suggested that if the federal government was going to subsidize subways, it should buy the lands around future stations at low pre-construction market prices. The government could then sell the parcels for development at their augmented post-subway value and return the profits to the taxpayers. This idea was not well-received. Being young and naïve, I did not grasp that

HUD's clients were not the taxpayers but the urban developers and their friends in state and municipal government, plus congressmen who could deliver the pork. A major purpose of this program, and of many others, was (and is) to create value with taxpayer money and then transfer it to the clients; in return, the clients support the agency by lobbying Congress and propagandizing the public.

The media remain mostly unmoved by these tales, and so does much of the public. The view seems to be that boys will be boys, and as long as all interests have a chance to shove their way to the trough the ultimate result will somehow be the general welfare of all of us.

Most government activity now consists of expenditures, laws and regulations, and taxes or tax exemptions adopted in response to special interest pressures. A small and shrinking share is devoted to the classic government functions of maintaining defense, supplying law and justice, providing public infrastructure, dispensing poor relief, and maintaining the conditions under which private initiative and free markets can flourish.

Neither common sense nor serious political theory supports the belief that this jostling of special interests will produce benign results. The economic analyses of the workings of the free market do not transfer to politics. In practice, the crises now roiling our economy and society are good evidence of the failure of the underlying assumptions that the clash of interest groups in the political marketplace can mimic the productive results of the clash of self-interest in the economic marketplace.

Big SIS, once it began growing, triggered a self-reinforcing feedback mechanism, and there is no off switch. Political analyst Jonathan Rauch described it over a decade ago in *Demosclerosis*:

Government's power to solve problems comes from its ability to reassign resources.... But that very ability energized countless investors and entrepreneurs and ordinary Americans to go digging for gold by lobbying government.... [T]the steady accumulation of subsidies and benefits, each defended in perpetuity by a professional interest group calcifies government.

The problem is not that special interests exist. As Madison knew, a tendency to form factions is built into human nature. Nor are factions necessarily bad. The pursuit of self-interest, alone or in concert with others, is the great engine of civilization. Abraham Lincoln once defended the patent system for "adding the fuel of interest to the fire of genius", and the principle holds broadly. The fuel of interest is essential to the workings of the economic system and to the web of non-market institutions called civil society.

Sometimes, the interaction of faction and government works out well, when the fuel of interest promotes the general welfare of the people. Recently, I drove the 2013 miles from Red Lodge, Montana, to Washington DC, almost entirely on the wonderful interstate highway system. (Well, it could use a bit of improvement north of Minneapolis.) Special interests had much to do with the system—truckers, shippers, contractors, workers, steel and concrete makers, real estate sharks, auto drivers, auto makers. Remove their energy, and I might still be sitting in traffic somewhere on the two lanes of the old US 30 that I rode on as a kid.

The problems arise when special interests expand their ambitions beyond calculating how to profit from legitimate and beneficial government actions. They come to regard capture of government as just another route to promoting private ends, regardless of any connection to legitimate governmental purposes.

If the lodestar of the general welfare is completely lost, then government programs turn into pure rapacity, as when bridges are built to nowhere, airports are subsidized to the tune of thousands of dollars per flight, high-speed rail is constructed based on fictional estimates of potential riders, and particular groups of citizens are singled out for special benefits or burdens.

Furthermore, a multiplier effect takes hold. As some groups succeed in capturing government, the incentives grow for others to take a run at it. The ultimate result is that government loses the capacity to say "no" and lets too many groups succeed in too big a way. The very multiplicity of demands prevents effective scrutiny, and the ability to adopt the interstate highway system and reject the bridges to nowhere is lost.

The result is a cascade of ever-increasing demands, often contradictory or mutually offsetting. A subsidizes B, who subsidizes C, who subsidizes A. Or even worse, A sends money to the government, which then sends it back to A, minus about 50 percent as a handling fee.

Not only are groups pitted against each other, but, because each of us belongs to many interests, fragments of ourselves are pitted against other fragments. I indignantly demand that the government protect me as a taxpayer against the damage caused by my success in lobbying for another of my interests.

Conflicts reach an insane level, as when the government subsidizes construction on flood plains, then passes environmental rules to prevent draining the land because it wants to protect water fowl. At one time, numerous government programs subsidized development on environmentally fragile barrier islands, terrain that should have remained pristine for both economic and environmental reasons. This was stopped by Ronald Reagan's administration, in a rare victory for common sense.

Complaints about Big SIS are often met with a shrug and a world-weary "it has always been this way". But this reaction is not correct, because for much of American history capture by special interests was regarded with horror, as documented in chapter 2.

And, to the extent that capture did exist in the past, its scale was much smaller. A system can tolerate some special interest capture when government controls 3 percent or 10 percent of the economy, as was true only a few generations ago. It breaks down when the government controls well over 50 percent of society's resources, as is the case today when you add up the costs of federal, state, and local government, plus the costs imposed by the regulatory system.

We have passed the point where special interest power can be dismissed as either a useful addition or minor irritation in a well-functioning political system. The current economic turmoil is largely the consequence of our embrace of Big SIS.

For a visual, consider Big SIS in terms of the mindless zombies of current popular culture. The zombies are finding gaps in the defenses of the democratic republic and are pouring through. The image is particularly apt because zombies are once-productive humans, now become predators. So it is with special interests, which are essential parts of society until they become fixated on feeding off of the government.

We need a broad collective recognition that the feeding frenzy has gone too far. We need a rollback, with new structures to prevent a recurrence. Each of us must forego government favoritism on the condition that others do the same. Such grand collective bargains are difficult to reach, at best, and they are difficult indeed when a binge has lasted a long time and has distorted the economy and society. Our politics lacks both theoretical and practical ideas on how to plug these gaps in the defenses of our civilization.

However, as the aphorism says, if something cannot go on, it will stop. Big SIS cannot go on, so it will stop. Whether it will power down and turn smoothly to a more sustainable course or crash into a solid wall is up to us.

"Crash" is not complete hyperbole, either. When Mancur Olson sought examples of the level of destruction necessary to overcome the sclerosis of special interest dominance, he thought of the World War II defeats of Germany and Japan and the Cultural Revolution in China. A recent economic study suggests that the Napoleonic invasion was a liberating force in the nineteenth century. The lack of examples of a smooth transition out of sclerosis is disheartening.

"The claim of a government to... obedience and loyalty"

In contemplating Big SIS, I am carried back five decades, and I see Professor Samuel Beer pacing the lecture hall stage at Harvard, thinking out loud. He is teaching Western Thought and Institutions, a course that became "legendary", according to his eventual *New York Times* obituary.

His topic is political legitimacy, which he defines as "the claim of a government to the obedience and loyalty of their citizens/subjects", and the underlying principles that determine how the right to make such a claim is gained and lost.

Throughout the year, the class time-travels to societies in crisis over legitimacy: England's anarchy of the twelfth century that led to the Magna Carta, and its revolutions of 1640–88; then on to Philadelphia in 1776; Paris in 1789; Lenin in St. Petersburg in 1917; and the end of the German Weimar Republic as Hitler became Chancellor in 1933. Later, Beer added a peaceful revolution: Britain in the nineteenth century, when it expanded the electorate and reformed its electoral districts.

The course only scratched the surface of the study of political legitimacy. An advanced session could examine the end of colonialism and the fall of the Soviet Empire. China's successive revolutions, including its current effort to perform the political equivalent of a triple flip without a net by shifting from one basis of legitimacy (Maoism) to a totally different one (economic development) without a violent interlude, would be worth intense examination, too.

Our advanced course should also focus on the United States in the early twenty-first century, where Big SIS is squandering legitimacy like a dissolute heir spending the fortune won by the hard work of his forebears. Big SIS is not simply a glitch in our politics that will be ironed out more or less routinely. Rather, the rise of Big SIS is due to some flaws in our fundamental political theories and practices, and its assault on the legitimacy of the republic is ominous.

Most of the people studied by Beer's time-traveling students did not understand the seriousness of their crises until quite late in the game, and we should take warning.

Preview of this book and what to do next Monday morning

This book develops the themes of the rise of Big SIS, its problems, and its relationship to the bedrock need of any political system for legitimacy.

Chapter 2 provides historical background, examining the political evolutions that produced the present Big SIS. Some of the choices made by our ancestors now appear unwise, but they seemed like good ideas at the time. We should look at their failures as experiments that did not work, and from which we can learn. The goal is not to return to some earlier political Eden but rather to go forward to renewed political arrangements that encompass the best lessons, and exclude the worst, of our collective experience.

The fundamental lesson is that the Founders built on three basic premises regarding the relationship of factions to government:

- That legislation should promote the general interest of the nation, not special interests;

- That systemic corruption—corruption that is then fed back into supporting the government—would rot the republic; and

- That the government could be a facilitator of many things but should not be regarded as being in charge of and responsible for any sector of the domestic economy or society. We must rely on our civilization, which is our market economy and civil society, not on our government.

The pressures of industrialization and depression caused us to shed these guiding principles. We need to recover them and adapt them to the current age.

Chapter 3 examines Big SIS as it exists today. The chapter begins with the old reliable "follow the money" approach, discussing budget, taxes, regulatory costs, and law. Then it examines broader effects on our economy and on the other institutions of civil society, as Big SIS has a disturbing habit of remaking everything it touches into its own image. The chapter closes with a collection of stories to illustrate why so many people are growing angry.

The conclusion is a dreary one. Big SIS is even bigger and more destructive than most people believe.

Chapter 4 contains both a diagnosis of the reasons for the current state of Big SIS and a prognosis. Why has the democratic republic become so vulnerable to the continuing expansion of Big SIS? What are the weaknesses that the zombies are exploiting? What is the outlook?

The lesson is somber. Momentum is not running in our favor.

Chapter 5 addresses possible solutions. Some good ideas are floating around, starting with the need to recognize the nature of the problem. Once we understand what has happened to us and why we need to recover the values of the Old Republic, many roads to reform open up.

The rise of the Tea Parties is a positive development because it demonstrates that people recognize the problems and are mobilizing themselves. The people are far ahead of the inside-the-beltway types in their willingness to face the realities of our national financial situation and act accordingly.

Escape from our dilemma will require sacrifice and compromise. I, in my various special-interest personas, will have to accept a haircut on what I regard as my just deserts. This need not be a big problem because I am an adult and know that the world is not fair, and I am willing to do my share. I also know that I personally will be better off with a smaller share of a bigger pie than I will be if everyone sticks hard to his or her maximum demands and produces stasis.

My acceptance is contingent, though, on others taking a haircut on their claims as well. In a society with so many special interests of so many kinds, this is hard to negotiate, but not impossible.

Specifically, I list eleven areas in which direct and productive action is both necessary and possible, and readers will undoubtedly come up with many additional ideas. People can do the following:

- Educate themselves and others about our problems: about Big SIS, the nature of political legitimacy, possibilities for productive collective action, and especially the need to return to three basic values of the Old Republic.

- Develop and support political candidates who are dedicated to reform.

- Slaughter the thousands of existing subsidies, both direct and via the tax system. Subsidies cannot be attacked piecemeal; there are too many.

- Pressure the representatives of our own special interests to be reasonable in their positions and to agree to haircuts in exchange for reciprocity from other interests.

- Appeal to the idealism in young congressional staffers, government workers, and members of the DC influence-peddling orbit—Big SIS is not a world in which they want to live, and embracing civic virtue is a healthy step toward a better world. Taking this step does not even require excessive idealism or self-sacrifice. It is in their own self-interest to open up their opportunities to lead lives of value and integrity.

- Pressure business as an institution to step up to defend the free market and reject crony capitalism.

- Bring the Regulatory State under control, starting by passing the buck of responsibility for regulations back to Congress.

- Coax the legal profession to recognize the realities of Big SIS and the rot in the governmental structures as they now exist.

- Jettison almost all campaign finance "reform" laws, which are actually mechanisms for enhancing the power of special interests at the expense of the citizenry.

- Return the medical system to the private market, with the government as facilitator and safety-net provider, not prime mover.

- Return to the convention system of nominating our presidential candidates.

Optimism about long term success is reasonable, but it should be tempered. As fans of the horror genre know, zombies do not give up easily, and neither will Big SIS. Those who see themselves as losers from reform will fight hard, and this group includes, unfortunately, a large portion of our so-called elites, who have comfortable careers as administrators of Big SIS, and who care little whether they possess political legitimacy as long as they can retain raw power.

Basic constitutional and institutional reform is a hard and messy business, and, while polities sometimes evolve peacefully, they often change only through appalling violence, as in the Civil War era, or, earlier, the American Revolution. We can reach the "sunlit uplands", using Winston Churchill's phrase, but the path that will take us there is uncertain and possibly stony.

Chapter Two

How We Got Here:
The Rise of Big SIS

Begin at the beginning. To understand the Big SIS of 2012, you must start with the founding of the American republic in the late eighteenth century and with Founders' fear of faction. You must then work your way through a couple of hundred years of history, examining how the Founders' principles for neutralizing faction have been applied (or ignored) in the changing circumstances of economic, political, and technological upheaval.

"Some common impulse of passion, or of interest"

To repeat Madison's definition, a faction is "a number of citizens, whether amounting to a majority or a minority of the whole, who are united and actuated by some common impulse of passion, or of interest, adversed to the rights of other citizens, or to the permanent and aggregate interests of the community."

Fear of faction was far from original with the Founders. A recurring problem in the history of human society is how to keep subgroups, whether called factions, special interests, distributional coalitions, or clients, from capturing the government and running it for their own benefit.

When the Israelites demanded a king to protect them, Samuel warned: "And he will take your fields, and your vineyards, and your oliveyards, even the best of them, and give them to his servants. And he will take the tenth of your seed, and of your vineyards, and give to his officers, and to his servants." (Most peasants, or contemporary middle-class Americans, would be delighted if the ruler and his minions took only a tenth.)

Medieval theorists addressed the fear of faction by developing elaborate concepts of the Great Chain of Being, with kings and aristocrats created naturally superior and virtuous by God, thus ruling the people for their own good. By definition, these were not factions because they were not concerned with their own interest; their political legitimacy came from God.

This theory does not hold up well when compared with reality. Thomas Paine's 1776 pamphlet *Common Sense*, which greatly influenced the political thought of the American Revolution, spoofed the idea of God-given kingly virtue. It described William, the Conqueror of Saxon Britain in 1066, as: "A French bastard landing with an armed Banditti and establishing himself king of England against the consent of the natives, is in plain terms a very paltry rascally original. It certainly hath no divinity in it."

Although the Founders were skeptical of monarchy, their solution was not pure democracy. No one ever thought this feasible except on a small scale because democracy turns quickly into ochlocracy—mob rule by shifting coalitions—and then into oligarchy and tyranny.

The best-known precedent, democratic Athens, was neither a reassuring model nor a long-lived state. However glorious in parts, it produced disastrous executions of good but unlucky commanders, a suicidal imperial adventure in Sicily, occasional genocide, and ultimate defeat by the Spartans and then the Macedonians. Its day was brief.

The Founders turned to the idea of a republic, a government based on the sovereignty of the people but with significant mediating institutions to prevent mob rule or transition into demagogic tyranny.

The decision for a republic was daring because there was little successful precedent for this form, either. The Roman Republic was primarily an oligarchy that became an autocracy, after degenerating into a century of bitter civil war.

The most recent example was the English Commonwealth from 1649 to 1660, after the civil war of the 1640s and the execution of Charles I. It was a republic of sorts that turned into military dictatorship and then into chaos. Another civil war appeared likely until a deal restored the Stuarts in exchange for the Act of Indemnity and Oblivion, and the conflict ended only after the Glorious Revolution of 1688 established parliamentary supremacy within a monarchial form.

In considering how to prevent a breakdown of a republic, Madison and his fellows accepted the existence of special interests as inevitable, as stated in *Federalist No. 10*: "latent causes of faction are…sown into the nature of man", and even "where no substantial occasion presents itself, the most frivolous and fanciful distinctions have been sufficient to…excite the most violent conflicts."

If faction could not be prevented, it had to be neutralized. Even better would be to harness faction to provide stability to the republic, and this is what the Founders set out to accomplish.

To succeed required that several risks be addressed.

The first risk was that particular minority factions would capture the new federal government and turn it into an instrument of their own.

This fear was well-grounded in experience, as capture by faction has been the fate of most governments throughout history. The obvious scenario is that a minority obtains control of the instruments of force, as aristocrats and kings controlled the force available in feudal society. This allows them to rule many times their number of commoners. As Clint Eastwood explains to Eli Wallach in *The Good, the Bad, and the Ugly*, "There's two kinds of people… those with loaded guns and those who dig—you dig."

Effective instruments of force must exist to protect against outside threats, so it is easy for their wielders to make themselves into the government, and into a leisure class that watches the peasants dig.

Another possibility is the development of a softer despotism. The government can get into the business of special interest favoritism and then use its patronage power to shore up its political power. The term of the time was "corruption", and it meant not just the petit larceny of bribes to officials but the grand larceny of hijacking the whole political system by creating economic advantages and then feeding part of the profits back into entrenching the political incumbents.

Historian John Joseph Wallis describes these two modes of corruption as "venal" and "systemic", and the latter was what really worried the Founders because it would destroy republican government. The danger was far from abstract in 1787, as British administration was shot through with systemic corruption. Half of the members of Parliament were under the control of the king, and Parliament created monopolies over crucial commodities, trading rights, and entire lines of business. Navigation Acts favored domestic shippers, and waves of enclosures appropriated common land for the benefit of the gentry.

The tea dumped into Boston Harbor on the night of December 16, 1773, belonged to the East India Company, a monopoly created by Parliament and one whose rack rents in India had contributed to ghastly famine in Bengal in 1770. Blurred by the patina of history, the Boston Tea Party looks like a bit of a frat-boy lark, but at the time it was deadly serious business.

Capture of government by a minority faction was not the only risk, nor did the Founders limit their concept of faction to minority subgroups of the nation.

An equal danger is a faction of the majority, which can then use the mechanisms of democracy to oppress the rest of the people. No minority will accept the legitimacy of such oppression forever, so control by majority faction is, in the long run, a guarantee of extra-legal conflict and even civil war.

In *Federalist No. 10*, which sets out the problem of a majority faction, there is no hint that the minority is wrong to rebel and no assumption that the majority has a right to oppress however it pleases, simply because it is a majority. The Founders were thinking within a tradition that held that no government had the right to take away people's God-given rights, such as life, liberty, and pursuit of happiness. Even kings could act so tyrannically as to forfeit their legitimacy, within medieval theory of the monarchy, and so could a majority, within the theory of republicanism.

To the Founders, the twentieth/twenty-first–century idea that a minority deserves no rights except those a whimsical majority chooses to grant would be totally mad. Contemporary political writers often say "elections have consequences", and so they do, but for the Founders these consequences did not include any right to loot or oppress the minority.

The Founders set out to perform a multiple balancing act among the threats posed by the different kinds of faction. They wanted to create a government strong enough to perform essential functions, such as defense, law, justice, and protection of commerce, but resistant to capture for parochial or tyrannical purposes by either minorities or majorities. Another famous line from *Federalist 51* is: "In framing a government…you must first enable the government to control the governed; and in the next place oblige it to control itself."

To read *The Federalist Papers* and other contemporary sources is to follow supple minds at work exploring and explaining the problems of setting interest against interest and ambition against ambition so that they check each other, and of setting limits on the powers of government that would limit the harm it could do even when factions did gain power.

The concern about a power grab by those controlling the instruments of force is dealt with in several ways.

Only Congress can declare war. The president cannot start a fight and then create an army that could threaten the republic. Congress also has the power to create and maintain a navy.

For the armed forces, the president is the commander-in-chief, but the main unit of the army is the militia, a term that includes the entire male population from which active forces can be drawn.

The Constitution reserves for the states the functions of training the militia and appointing the officers. This restriction means that no general or president who is acting against the republic can count on the loyalty of the state-appointed colonels. Nor, because of that subtle decision to make training a state function, can a federal general automatically count on the sergeants, who will also be drawn from the states. The Founders understood that the sergeants are the linchpin of any army.

As a backup, there is the Second Amendment: "A well regulated Militia, being necessary to the security of a free State, the right of the people to keep and bear Arms, shall not be infringed."

So, the first line of defense against military coup is that the generals cannot count on the loyalty of the colonels or sergeants. If this safety device fails, the colonels cannot count on the loyalty of the citizen-troops; in addition, there are many other citizens who are familiar with arms but not part of the active army.

These layered provisions deliberately keep the possibility of rebellion alive. The Founders were not squeamish about armed resistance to capture by faction. Judge Alex Kozinski recently put it as follows:

The Second Amendment is a doomsday provision, one designed for those exceptionally rare circumstances where all other rights have failed—where the government refuses to stand for reelection and silences those who protest; where courts have lost the courage to oppose, or can find no one to enforce their decrees. However improbable these contingencies may seem today, facing them unprepared is a mistake a free people get to make only once.

Preventing political, as opposed to military, power grabs presented a different set of problems. *Federalist 51* lays out the thinking behind a complex structure designed to forestall capture by a minority, a majority, or any coalition in between.

The first safeguard is that sovereignty is split between federal and state governments. The "power allotted" is then subdivided among separate departments. "The different governments will control each other, at the same time that each will be controlled by itself."

The second protection is the natural fragmentation of society into "so many parts, interests, and classes of citizens, that the rights of individuals, or of the minority, will be in little danger from interested combinations of the majority" because "a coalition of a majority of the whole society could seldom take place on any other principles than those of justice and the general good."

These provisions of *Federalist No. 51* are described as "defense in depth" by the Claremont Institute's William Voegeli:

> Majorities will be transient coalitions of many small factions, respecting the rights of the minority not for high-minded reasons, but out of awareness that the next coalition formed to address the next issue could leave a faction that belongs in today's majority in tomorrow's minority.

Many commenters have observed that the system established in the Constitution makes action slow, difficult, and sometimes impossible.

These observations are true, but skewed. The Constitution defines the enumerated powers, those that encompass the essential core of government actions, clearly enough. Over the centuries, political operators have found the levers of action adequate when national defense and survival were at stake, especially because crises create public willingness to stretch the boundaries and accelerate action. Usually, the end of the crisis has meant a return to normalcy, as happened after the Civil War and World War I.

The checks and balances that slow the pace of action are designed to resist capture of the government by any faction or demagogue, which is hardly a bad thing. Delay is designed into the system as a feature, not a bug, to prevent actions that the Founders thought the government should not be taking anyway.

Charles Evans Hughes, who was almost elected president in 1916 and was chief justice in the 1930s, called the Constitution "the greatest instrument ever designed to prevent things from being done." Justice Antonin Scalia delivered a rejoinder to a Senate committee in 2011: "Americans…should learn to love the gridlock. It's there so the legislation that does get out is good legislation."

The limits on the powers and speed of governmental action were related to an unstated assumption. No one thought of the government as being "in charge" of the economy or society, or as being responsible for everything.

Over the years, many debates took place over the role of government in facilitating other sectors, such as manufacturing or agriculture or transportation, but no one assigned *primacy* to the government. If the government was only a potential facilitator of ongoing processes, then slowness of action was not debilitating. Any evils caused by delay were offset by the importance of providing time for debate and for the forces of republican virtue to make themselves felt.

The Constitution, the constitution, and political legitimacy

These fears of the effects of faction reverberated through the nineteenth century and provided boundaries on what people accepted as legitimate government actions.

A distinction needs to be drawn between the Constitution of the United States and the term "constitution" in a general sense. They are not the same thing, but both are crucial to understanding the structure and legitimacy of government and the evolution of Big SIS.

Our cornerstone as a political entity remains the revered "The Constitution" of 1787 as improved, particularly by the Bill of Rights and the Civil War–era amendments.

But there is also a broader national constitution. The definition of "constitution" is "the system of fundamental laws and principles that prescribes the nature, functions, and limits of a government or another institution." Some authors use the terms "constitutional order" or "regime", defined by scholar Mark Tushnet as "a reasonably stable set of institutions through which a nation's fundamental decisions are made over a sustained period, and the principles that guide those decisions."

These broader terms remind us that the Constitution is short and often cryptic and that it rests on a foundation of assumptions and practices that are not spelled out in the document itself. An example: safeguarding property rights is important in the Constitution, yet the word is nowhere defined. The nature of property is left to the background principles of law. Another: the right of *habeas corpus* is protected but is nowhere defined. The Constitution accepts it as already extant in the common law.

The whole Constitution follows this pattern. Its specific provisions rest on a foundation of public beliefs and practices about government and rights that arise out of history and culture.

To understand the overall constitutional order of any time and place, including our own, requires attention to its broader underlying principles as well as to the bare words of a formal Constitution. These underlying principles, not just the formal words, are crucial to the political legitimacy of a government's "claim…to the obedience and loyalty of their citizens/subjects", in Professor Beer's definition. The foundational assumptions, not just the topmost part of the structure called "The Constitution", determine how a government's claim to legitimacy can be gained or lost.

The concept of legitimacy receives too little attention in current political discourse. It includes more than the idea of bare legality. To say a government is legitimate means that the people accept it as having a sound moral basis and believe that it embodies their collective sense of fair play and justice. One can regard as legitimate even a decision with which one disagrees when one accepts that the government had a right to make it and that the proper procedures were followed.

On the other hand, pure power and procedure are not enough, and a decision is not legitimate if the action exceeds a polity's deep sense of the limits of proper government action. As the aphorism has it, great changes should not be forced by slender majorities.

Even beneficiaries of a decision may regard it as lacking legitimacy, although, like an athlete profiting from a blown referee's call, they usually shut up. Nonetheless, sharp practice undermines the legitimacy of the system even in the minds of the immediate winners.

A pervasive problem in contemporary Washington is the contempt of the political classes for the idea that there is such a thing as political legitimacy that goes beyond immediate election results or the latest parliamentary maneuvering.

Nor should one be too legalistic in assessing legitimacy. Another problem in contemporary Washington is that lawyers, including those on the Supreme Court, are often overly clever, focusing on logic-chopping and oblivious to the interplay between the Constitution and the constitution.

Lawyers think legitimacy rests on their ability to exhume past Supreme Court language to find support for governmental power, and then say "Aha—under the 1942 case of *Wickard v. Filburn* and Footnote 4 of 1938's *Carolene Products*, the federal government can do anything it damn well pleases, so yes the Commerce Clause says the government can make you eat broccoli. We win!"

Common sense—the constitution—replies with Charles Dickens that "if the law supposes that, then the law is an ass." Eating broccoli is not commerce, and for a court to say it is does not make it so. A famous Lincoln anecdote has him asking, "If you call a tail a leg, how many legs has a dog?" When the answer "five" comes back, Lincoln said: "No, four, because calling a tail a leg does not make it one."

If the Supreme Court has twisted itself into a linguistic knot that renders the limitations embodied in the Constitution pointless, the effect is not to lend legitimacy to its decisions. Quite the opposite; when the contortions transgress the constitution and political legitimacy, they undermine the legitimacy of the Court as an institution.

As a lawyer, I was blindsided by the strong popular reaction against the Supreme Court's 2005 *Kelo* decision, which upheld the use of eminent domain to tear down perfectly good homes for the purpose of creating an economic development district. The outcome was within the Supreme Court precedents, which deferred to the decisions of local governments about the validity of the public purposes for which eminent domain is used. My reaction was "nothing new in this one".

The public had not read the precedents, had not known how far the law had gone in giving unlimited authority to local governments, and thought "this just isn't right!" The damage to the legitimacy of the Supreme Court was considerable and was compounded recently by the news that the development project has gone belly-up. The land on which Ms. Kelo's lovingly-tended home once stood is now a waste dump.

The Supreme Court's legitimacy continues to be damaged by the *Kelo* decision, as the Internet disseminates the truth about the deep systemic corruption and cronyism that is rampant at state redevelopment agencies. Only the Court seems oblivious, occupying an insulated fantasy world of wise and disinterested public servants rather than the grubby reality of local corruption.

In the end, the Constitution may be what the Supreme Court says it is, but this is not necessarily true of the broader constitution, which draws from many wellsprings. A rough benchmark of political legitimacy is the sense of what it right and fit, so if you do not like Dickens, then go with Kipling:

The Saxon is not like us Normans.
His manners are not so polite.
But he never means anything serious
till he talks about justice and right.
When he stands like an ox in the furrow
with his sullen set eyes on your own,
And grumbles, "This isn't fair dealing,"
my son, leave the Saxon alone.

"Fear of corruption verging on paranoia": the Old Republic

Throughout the nineteenth century, one of the great foundation stones of the underlying constitutional order, and a constant subject of political discourse, was the concern about "corruption", harking back to the web of special privileges, court favorites, offices, monopolies, and other benefits that the Crown, or, in the colonies, a royal governor, could bestow on supporters.

As Wallis wrote with respect to the concept of "systematic corruption" used to bind the recipients to the government with the objective of dominating that government:

> [F]ear of corruption verging on paranoia, became a dominant feature of American politics in the early 19th century. In the process, the rhetoric of corruption emerged as the common grammar of politics, so overwhelming that it became difficult to discuss public questions in any other language.... [T]he word most often brought to mind a fuller, more coherent, and more dreadful image of a spreading rot. A frequent metaphor compared corruption to organic cancer, eating at the vitals of the body politic and working a progressive dissolution.

An example demonstrating the continuing vitality of this fear is that during the Wisconsin Constitutional Convention of 1846, a delegate proposed to prohibit all banks on the ground that legislatures were vulnerable to their bribery and undue influence. The measure passed, 79-27.

That provision did not survive, but the delegate seems to have been a shrewd judge of the state officials. In 1857, several companies competed in Wisconsin for the federal land grants available for railroad construction. The award was overturned when it became known that the winner had given $50,000 worth of stock to the governor, $10,000 to the chief justice and other state officials, and smaller amounts to more than half of the members of the legislature.

Obviously, the Founders' pessimism about humanity's propensity for corruption was realistic. Of course, you can pick your narrative for the Wisconsin stories: the evil banks and railroads tempting the upright public officials, or the corrupt public officials auctioning off their power to the helpless businesses. The narrative of Big SIS can be a tale of extortion as well as bribery.

Closely related to a horror of corruption was a fear of class-based or special-interest legislation. The Founders took seriously the idea that laws should promote the general welfare. The Constitution's enumerated powers are all directed along these lines, and the structure of setting faction against faction and power against power is designed to ensure that the levers of power that must exist if a government is to accomplish anything will be used "to promote the general Welfare", as the preamble to the Constitution puts it, not seized by any faction for private advantage.

Again, the Founders were realistic about the innate human capacity for greed and sin. During one of the many nineteenth-century debates over government financing of internal improvements, such as roads and canals, North Carolina political leader Nathaniel Macon said:

> The great question now in North Carolina must be whether or not we are to approve a wild and profligate scheme of Internal Improvements, adopted by an abominable system of log-rolling and deception—the result of which is to impose taxation to the amount of five times what we now pay.

He had a good point. In the 1830s and 1840s, many of the sponsors of bills to help turnpikes and railroads happened to own land in the towns to be served.

Nonetheless, and despite the concerns, between 1790 and 1860, state and local governments spent $450 million—and the federal government another $60 million—financing transportation projects. The results were not good, as few of the government investments paid off and many states endured financial crises and defaults in the 1830s and 1840s.

The experience hardened the resistance of later generations to the evils of special-interest legislation. Barriers were erected by social norms, electoral threats, and legislative caution, and were enforced by courts. Many state constitutions (as well as the Fifth Amendment to the U.S. Constitution) referred to "due process" or "the law of the land". Courts ruled that these clauses required that laws be general and impartial and prohibited legislation designed to burden or benefit particular people or factions.

The judicial resistance to faction was widespread. By 1868, courts in at least twenty of the thirty-seven states endorsed some version of a requirement that legislation be for the general welfare. In an 1898 Supreme Court case involving special liabilities imposed on railroads, a lawyer filed a 109-page survey of the case law on "restrictions against unequal, partial, or class legislation". The brief added references to histories that said one cause of the ratification of the Constitution was "the outrageous, partial, and unjust legislation" passed by states in the 1780s under the Articles of Confederation.

Such a requirement of public benefit is anathema to the governing classes of the current day. Standard contemporary legal doctrine brands it as "substantive due process" and regards it as intolerable judicial arrogance. But the need for public benefit was a crucial part of the thinking that produced the original Constitution, as reinforced by the problems with government financing of internal improvements in the nineteenth century.

Dominant constitutional thinking in the nineteenth century also found an implicit limit on taxing power. Expenditures had to be for "public purposes", not private benefit. The definition allowed governments to pay for basic public goods, and included charitable relief on the approved list. As the Supreme Court said in 1881:

> Taxes for schools, for the support of the poor, for protection against fire, and for water-works, are the specific taxes found in the list complained of. We think it will not be denied by any one that these are public purposes in which the whole community have an interest, and

for which, by common consent, property owners everywhere in this country are taxed.

Congress agreed about charity. It regularly voted to give aid to areas hit by natural disasters—almost 150 times between 1790 and 1930—but it routinely required reassurance that the recipients had not caused their own misfortune.

Rules against class legislation present obvious problems of enforcement. The boundaries between governmental actions to promote the general welfare and those that further parochial interests are rarely clear, and actions that promote general welfare inevitably help some people more than others. A particular road may be an excellent idea for the public benefit, but the paving industry will still profit the most.

Nonetheless, a doctrine that only general welfare legislation should pass provides considerable protection, not just in court but by framing political debate.

For example, protective tariffs are easily cited as an example of gross special-interest favoritism, During the nineteenth century, though, Henry Clay tried hard to sell them as advantageous to all, not just to manufacturers. He entitled his 1832 speech defending tariffs "The American System", and directed his considerable rhetorical and conciliatory talents at persuading the South Carolinians that the system as a whole worked in their interest, not just in that of the manufacturers. He included a blizzard of figures supporting the proposition that protecting American manufactures increased competition, which then lowered prices.

The Carolinians remained unconvinced, and the controversy led to the great Nullification Crisis of 1833, when South Carolina declared the tariff null and void within the state, relenting only after considerable compromise was accepted.

More difficulties in enforcing a doctrine that laws must promote the general welfare are created by the political reality of log-rolling. This custom can be a useful device through which the government invests in a portfolio of projects, each of which appeals to a minority but which in sum create substantial and general public benefits. On the other hand, log-rolling can enable greedy but small factions to coalesce into a majority to loot the rest of the polity. Or it can do both. In Ohio in the 1820s to 1840s, two useful canals were built, and then politics demanded support for eight more canals, twenty-six turnpikes, and six railroads, most of which were unprofitable and a few of which were frauds.

In some ways, things do not change much: in the 1970s, when Congress enacted a bill to clean up hazardous waste sites it specified that every state must have at least one such site, thus proving that no pork is too tainted. An objective observer might think that a state would prefer *not* to need any hazardous waste cleanup, but this is not the logic of pork-barrel log-rolling.

Log-rolling creates a dangerous gap in the Founders' system of defences against factions and special interest laws, and a puzzling one. They were certainly aware of the phenomenon, which presents obvious weaknesses in Madison's theory that factions would be too numerous to allow the creation of a tyranny of the majority. But the constitutional structure contains no effective check, and the *Federalist 51* discussion of the point seems almost—dare one say it?—naïve.

Perhaps the Founders knew that the only serious defence to evil outcomes from log-rolling lies in limits on the overall reach of government. If government power is unlimited, then the possibilities for log-rolling coalitions of looters will become overwhelming.

The Old Republic in the Post-Civil War Era

The questions of general welfare versus particular interests could not be answered in the abstract. Specific instances were the stuff of year-to-year politics. The nineteenth century was full of contentious debate over tariffs, internal improvements, public-domain lands, the transcontinental railroad, research on agricultural improvements, the patent system, disaster relief, Civil War pensions, and legal treatment of strikes. (There was also, of course, debate over slavery, which was outside any system of normal politics.)

On the other hand, the fact that grey exists is not a convincing argument that black and white do not. In many cases, it was hard to tell whether special or general interests were being served, but that does not negate the fact that other cases were clearly far over on one side or the other. They were clearly for the public benefit or clearly abuses.

Allowing for the difficulty of many of the specific issues, it is safe to say that the Founders' constitution—call it the Old Republic—including their concepts of how to avoid destruction by faction, remained in good order in the post-Civil War Era. The assumptions remained that political legitimacy involved an abhorrence of corruption, especially of the systemic variety; a ban on special-interest legislation combined with a safety valve for some public goods and charity; and a belief that the government was not in charge of society or the economy.

Another reality of the day was that governments were not big spenders. Hard battles over government policy took place, but as late as 1902 all governments in the United States spent only 7 percent of the Gross National Product. Of this, most (3.5 percent) occurred at the local level, states spent 0.76 percent, and the Feds controlled 2.71 percent. The opportunities for special interest rapine were bounded.

However, under the pressures of population increase, industrialization, and nationalization (using this term as a parallel to the current "globalization"), the practical application of the principles grew increasingly difficult.

For example, as the railroad and the telegraph transformed the United States into a national market, the economic changes put severe pressures on local economic actors and created serious incentives for them to demand that state and local governments help them cheat the out-of-towners.

The Supreme Court decided over three hundred cases on municipal bond financing during the late nineteenth century. Local governments sought to attract railroad investment with offers of aid in the form of bond issues, ignoring provisions against such bonds in state constitutions. Often, they got judicial blessing for the bond issue. The bonds would be sold to Wall Street or to foreign investors and would then be repudiated, again with the blessing of state courts, which characterized the earlier approval as an unfortunate error.

As scholar Michael Greve notes: "The liquidity and marketability of commercial paper in secondary markets depended on ensuring the integrity of the underlying transactions. And only the Supreme Court could provide that protection." So it did, overruling the state repudiations.

This theme of local resistance to the relentless push for national and worldwide access to capital, markets, and industrialization kept recurring.

The federal government held to the policy that it would not allow the states to cripple private actions directed at developing national markets. This principle was applied in the context of the refrigerated meat car, the sewing machine, and a host of other businesses. Local authorities were ingenious at inventing new ways to burden commerce for the benefit of their constituents, and courts met the challenge with equal ingenuity. They crafted doctrines to give the locals adequate power to meet valid concerns while blocking their efforts to exclude or loot outsiders.

These same doctrines sometimes protected minorities against local animus, based on the doctrine that the Fourteenth Amendment "protected the right to earn a livelihood free of unreasonable government interference". But often they failed, as the Supreme Court refused to enforce the guarantee of "privileges and immunities" in the Fourteenth Amendment, and left African Americans at the mercy of racist state governments.

Much of the agenda protecting national markets against local depredation was administered by the Supreme Court, but it was not a judicial idiosyncrasy. It represented a clear political policy supported by the dominant forces of the time, a part of the constitution as well as the Constitution.

With it went the principle that the national government would not cripple commerce, either. The name given the policy was "laissez faire", and the historians and political activists of the Progressive Era, the New Deal, and the Great Society sneered that it was an abdication of governmental responsibility and a corrupt sellout to large corporations.

This interpretation is propaganda. The literal translation of "laissez faire" is "let do", which means it was a policy of permitting business to produce dynamic economic expansion. The hands-off policy did not give business the easy life of the rentier. Indeed, the ideology of laissez faire was to protect interstate commerce from rentiers in the form of local barons and existing vested interests that captured the mechanisms of local governments.

This focus on dynamism is crucial to understanding the deference given to property rights and contracts during the late nineteenth century. I was once privileged to talk with Hernando de Soto, the brilliant Peruvian advocate of the need for better protection of property rights in the third world. He commented that anywhere south of the equator, "property rights" means "protect the rich" in possession of their estates. However, the rich may well prefer a static society in which they live on *latifundios* surrounded by a servile class of peasants, and they may use their property rights to retard economic growth rather than foster it. The term "property rights" does not carry with it American society's assumption that these will be used in the service of economic dynamism.

What would have been the result of an opposite policy, one that gave the states freedom to deal with national businesses as they chose? Paul Freund, my Constitutional Law professor at Harvard half a century ago, found this an easy question. To see what the United States would look like without the protections given national commerce by our Constitution, one need only examine the liquor industry. When the Prohibition Amendment was repealed, the states were given carte blanche to regulate booze as they willed, and the result was a web of local protectionism, favoritism, exploitation, corruption, and inefficiency.

The courts could use the values of the Old Republic to battle the efforts of local interests and local government against the nationalization of commerce, but other issues were harder to sort out.

Industrialization, urbanization, and increasing population density caused novel problems, and governments were regarded as the only institutions capable of dealing with them.

The new, large-scale industries needed workers, which meant they located in cities. This produced population density, because the workers walked to work. In eighteen states, three-quarters of the manufacturing was urban-based and produced waste, pollution, and annoyance on a large scale.

U.S. population grew more than 350 percent between 1850 and 1920, and urbanization increased apace. In 1880,

71 percent of Americans were rural; in 1920, the urbanites were a majority for the first time.

The horsecar helped to disperse workers and factories somewhat, but the new densities created immense problems.

Take the homely example of animal waste. Three million horses lived in urban areas in the late nineteenth century. The twenty-five pounds of manure and gallon of urine per day produced by each might be beneficial as fertilizer on a farm, but not as waste deposited on the streets of cities or in manure pits of stables near residential areas. Anyone who objects to the air pollution from autos should be sent back to an 1890s summer in New York to breathe in the rich mix of dust and powdered manure. Nor were the products of live horses the only disposal problem; in 1880, New York City scavengers collected 15,000 dead ones.

Garbage in general was a huge issue. In a rural area, waste disposal is easy. In a city, it is a challenge. In the 1890s, Chicago collected 2000 cubic yards of refuse each day, and New York clogged the approaches to the harbor by dumping its garbage in the Atlantic.

A Libertarian would say that these and many other issues of urban interaction could be handled by common law, contract, and evolving common-law legal institutions, and he or she would have a point. But given the pace of change in the nineteenth century, the problems grew far faster than institutions to deal with them.

Sanitation *had* been a private matter until well into the nineteenth century, and it was the breakdown of this mode that created the pressures for government to act. The urban dweller in the new industrial age, whether he embraced the old "miasma" theory of disease or adopted the newfangled thinking that blamed germs, was not disposed to patience.

Governments needed to be able to use what is called "the police power", and no theory of the Constitution or the constitution has ever denied the need and power of governments to deal with the infinite variety of public health, safety, and general friction issues that arise in the course of human affairs.

In this area, the boundary between general welfare and special-interest laws can never be better than rough and ready; perfection is not necessary as long as there is a general commitment to restraint, and obeisance to general welfare principles, even if people try to cheat at the margins.

The need for law

Industrialization challenged the Old Republic from another direction. The new industries needed government and law, and on a big scale.

Railroads and utilities must acquire rights-of-way. To avoid holdouts by strategically placed property owners, they needed to borrow the government's power of eminent domain. These were also regarded as natural monopolies, which meant that there was room for only one company in a given area, so they needed government franchises to protect them against competition.

The new industries, especially the railroad, raised knotty and novel legal issues. Who bears the loss from damage caused by smoke and sparks from locomotives? (The answer: for ordinary emissions, the adjoining landowner; for smoke that collects in a tunnel and is then released in a cloud, the railroad.) Who should pay for fencing to separate cattle and railroads? (A saying of the time: "nothing increases the value of a cow like crossing it with a speeding locomotive.") What rules should govern road/rail crossings? (That is, should trains have to stop to look for road vehicles or vice versa?) If a negligent worker injures another worker, is the employer liable for the damage? (Answer: first no, then yes.)

Later propagandists of the Progressive Era and the New Deal mocked the frequently close relations between big business and legislatures, classifying everything as corrupt. This stance is reductionist. Laws to facilitate commerce and production are well within any reasonable definition of the general welfare, and the liberal propagandists made and make no distinction between these and special-interest corruption. Their goal was to delegitimize business and commerce, clearing the way for an expanded government that controlled and dominated rather than facilitated the private sector.

The issues are hard, because the need for franchises and laws certainly created opportunities for corruption at all levels. The Wisconsin bribery case in the 1850s was not unusual. In 1874, Collis P. Huntington, one of the California Big Four who built the Central Pacific Railroad, instructed an agent to send someone to Arizona to get a franchise from the legislature. He cautioned: "It would not do to have it known that we had any interest in it, for the reason it would cost us much more money to get such a bill through if it was known it was for us."

In the same letter, Huntington fretted about the upcoming session of the U.S. Congress and the amount that rival Tom Scott might be willing to pay to get a bill through for his Texas Pacific Railroad. Huntington did not think Scott would succeed, but he worried because: "I think this coming session of Congress will be composed of the hungriest sort of men that ever got together, and the d____ only knows what they will do."

Clearly, the needs of the rising industrial state were at the center of politics, and purity was in short supply on all sides. During the disputed presidential election of 1876, with the future of Reconstruction hanging in the balance and amid justified fear of armed violence and renewed rebellion, an issue in the negotiation pot was the franchise of the Texas Pacific Railroad.

The five Chicago Aldermen of the 1890s were called "the gray wolves", and they earned the name.

As with Wisconsin, you can pick your narrative. The usual story, reinforced by the pro-Big SIS propagandists of the Progressive Era, the New Deal, and the Great Society, is a tale of evil businessmen corrupting innocent public officials, as if they were introducing a bunch of country boys to the House of the Rising Sun. A different theory is that political entrepreneurs built and ran the House of the Rising Sun, understanding the value of what they had to sell and extracting the maximum for their governmental services from businessmen who had no choice except to pay to play.

Huntington's letter about the Arizona franchise represents my preferred narrative—the can-do business tycoon with his world-weary tolerance dealing with office-holding parasites who hold him up even as he tries to benefit their constituents. But mine is a minority view.

A puzzle of the era is the scandal over the financing of the Union Pacific railroad. It became *the* great example of the Gilded Age, the foundation myth of the left to this day. Yet, from the documents of the time, the costs of construction look pretty much in line with the costs of other lines, and the peculiar financing was compelled by the corporate structure that Congress imposed on the Union Pacific and other transcontinental railroads. This great founding myth of Progressivism looks like a fraud. This would not be the last time that the anti-business left invented its facts.

The mystery about the Union Pacific financing leads to a larger point, which is that it is hard to know the importance or breadth of corruption during the late nineteenth century.

Mark Twain, who coined the term *The Gilded Age* as a book title, made his living as a teller of tall tales. The book is amused in tone, not bitter, and if Twain was offended by the opulence of the era and the scramble for wealth, he hid it well. In 1874, the publication year, he moved into a nineteen-room mansion, and in 1881 he retained Louis Tiffany as his interior designer.

The corruption narrative served so many interests, and a few anecdotes have been repeated so often that "everybody knows" it must be so. Some degree of corruption there certainly was (i.e., Huntington's letters), but a conclusion about its scale, motivations, and importance deserves a large question mark. It is unlikely that it approached anything like the scale of corruption in the United States at the turn of the twentieth/twenty-first centuries. The entrepreneurs of the Gilded Age at least built railroads; in more recent years, the doyens of the government-sponsored mortgage associations engaged in massive bribery to appropriate for themselves one-third of the value of the government subsidies for Fannie and Freddie. The corruption of the green energy racket dwarfs the most grandiose ambitions of the railroad builders.

In general, the corruption of the period seems to fit Wallis' concept of venal corruption rather than republic-threatening systemic corruption. Huntington did not get a monopoly from Arizona; he only paid for the opportunity to build useful infrastructure. Throughout the great railroad boom of the nineteenth century, the problem was *not* that railroads were given lucrative monopolies on the East India Company model. It was that railroads were overbuilt to the point where profits were unobtainable, and they went bankrupt.

Networks, platforms, and the nationalization of industry

The rise of the railroad also intensified the big question that surrounds internal improvements generally—who pays and who benefits?

The name we now give to enterprises such as railroads is "network". The term describes any large-scale, far-flung enterprise, but most of the hard problems arise when a network provides a platform on which other, smaller economic actors must rely. The railroads were the leading example because the shippers lived or died with railroad access and rates. More recent examples of platforms are the Internet connections of the telecommunications companies, Microsoft's operating system, Google's search engine, and the iPod/iPad.

A network industry often has high fixed-capital costs and low operating costs. To build a railroad and run the first train over it might cost a billion dollars. To run the second train adds only the cost of some more cars, the crew's wages, and fuel. This characteristic creates tough problems. Where the railroad faces competition, it will cut price to the bone, making just a bit over the operating costs. Then it will try to collect enough revenue to pay its capital costs by jacking up rates in areas where it has no competition.

The relationship between the railroads and their users was bound to be prickly. A railroad is worth zero without traffic, which in the nineteenth-century West meant farms and mines. On the other hand, farmland or mineral resources were worth zero without a railroad to move the product to market. Together, they could make beautiful music.

The problem, then and now, is how to split the financial returns. The railroad wanted to charge the farmers as much as possible, to the point where they were working as subsistence-level peasants. It also wanted to discriminate in rates, charging the most wherever it had the least competition. The farmers wanted to lure the railroad into building the network and then force it to charge only the minimum necessary for operations—the incremental cost of the crews and fuel. In this model, the farmers would get to steal the value of the railroad's original investment.

There is no neat solution to these conflicting aims. One approach is to integrate the activities, perhaps by giving the railroad grants of land along the right-of-way, which it can then sell off for a price that reflects the value added by transportation. This was done on a large scale. (Note that this is similar to the issues presented by the HUD-financed subways mentioned in the Introduction. It is amusing when people criticize the land grants to railroads while endorsing the taxpayer rip-offs inherent in contemporary subsidies to mass transit.)

Another approach was to have the future shippers finance a rail line. Local businesses knew that any town bypassed by the rail network was doomed to wither, and the number of lines built during the nineteenth century grew far beyond the needs of the available traffic. Much of the overbuilding was paid for by the local shippers.

When the activities of production and transportation are not integrated, there is no obvious answer to the revenue split. An economics text will show the range of possible outcomes: the farmers will not work for less than subsistence, and the railroad will not run for less than in its operating costs. Within this broad range, the outcome will depend on the relative abilities of the parties to bargain, bluff, threaten, and endure economic pain. It will be highly situation-specific.

Because of these inherent problems, the history of late nineteenth century railroading is one of outraged railroad tycoons complaining about shippers, angry shippers attacking railroads, railroads overbuilding so that none of them could make any money, and government officials arbitrating between them while auctioning off their own considerable ability to do favors. In addition, there is Michael Greve's account of the municipal bond frauds.

The result, after a couple of decades of upheaval and railroad bankruptcies, was the creation of the Interstate Commerce Commission in 1887, the first of what would become a mighty armada of regulatory agencies.

Historians once taught that the ICC was the instrument that brought the rapacious railroads under control, but this is simplistic. The railroads would have preferred private cartels, but if these were not workable then they also needed the ICC, and its function was to protect railroads from shippers and from each other as much as it was to protect shippers. The overbuilt railroads needed a mechanism to avoid the hell of watching competition drive rates down to their operating costs while the value of their capital investments shriveled. Uber-banker J. P. Morgan, the premier railroad financier of the era, was skeptical of the Commission, but once it was created he became a leader of the efforts to make it useful.

The ICC was also an apple in the Garden of Eden in that it was the first step towards an administrative Regulatory State, one in which great power is delegated to sub-units of the government. This evolution has been crucial to the evolution of Big SIS, as shall be taken up at the end of this chapter.

Another source of heavy pressure on the idea of neutral government came from labor. While average wages increased and working hours began their long trend downward, the myth arose that has continued to this day—that employers had great power over their workers and that they used it to exploit them.

In sorting out this claim, the baseline is that the nineteenth century was a hard place, and few modern Americans would want to live there, however interesting it is to visit.

Take the telling detail of attitudes toward horses, which were treated unsentimentally as machines. Mary Livermore, who helped establish nursing services during the Civil War, wrote of her experience with the Union Army in Tennessee, which had one horse or mule for every four men. She saw animals that got stuck in the mud and were left to die there, with no one even bothering to shoot them. In the 1890s, the average life span of a working horse in New York City was four years, as animals were systematically overworked and underfed. It is difficult for us to recapture or understand this mind-set.

So some employers might regard the workers as the equivalent of livestock, to be used and then sent to the glue factory, and an important part of the national story is the steady change in attitudes on this. Of course, it was a religious age, and other employers saw themselves as having deep duties toward their fellows, including workers.

The evolving attitudes toward the workforce did not necessarily mean that government action was required. The treatment of workers in industry reflected the reality that the jobs, however unpleasant they appear in modern eyes, were better than working on a nineteenth-century farm or in whatever part of Europe the workers had emigrated from.

The changing attitudes were also reflected in what workers would accept, and wages and working conditions improved under the lash wielded by the invisible hand of the market. Between 1900 and 1930, a time when the Progressive Movement was steadily battering at the need to protect workers from ruthless capitalists, the market treated workers quite well. Child labor declined from 6 percent to 1.4 percent of the workforce, and average hours worked per week shrank by 15 percent while hourly wages tripled. Overall pay went up by a factor of 2.58, outstripping the 100 percent inflation of 1900–30.

Nonetheless, as Professor David Bernstein says, "[T]he implicit assumption [was] that market outcomes were unfair to all but the wealthy and corporate interests, who benefitted at the expense of the rest of society."

Bernstein finds this puzzling: "Given consistently rising standards of living for workers during the heyday of American capitalism, when government support for labor unions was minimal, the roots of this belief are obscure."

Howard Gillman, a leading scholar of the era, makes a persuasive case that the judicial decisions upholding laws governing employment relations did not represent a rejection of the basic taboo against class legislation. He argues that the courts maintained the principle but adopted a more complex view of the meaning of "general welfare", accepting the rhetoric of the time about the existence of undue corporate power and bargaining imbalances that justified an "even-the-scales" approach. The government could legitimately take the part of one set of interests in society against another "to ensure that labor markets functioned properly and to redress inequalities of bargaining power", in Bernstein's phrase.

Perhaps so, but the change is momentous nonetheless because "equalize the bargaining power" is a rationale with no obvious limits. It can be plugged in to support any instance of the government taking the part of a special interest in its commercial disputes with other interests.

More pressure on the assumptions of the Old Republic came from fear of "the trusts". John Sherman, author of the first of the antitrust laws, said, "If we will not endure a king as a political power we should not endure a king over the production, transportation, and sale of any of the necessaries of life."

As with so much other nineteenth-century history, conventional teaching on this issue is dubious.

In general, from 1880 to 1890, real gross domestic product grew by 24 percent while output in supposedly monopolized industries grew by 175 percent. In the popular mind, the greatest symbol of the evil trust was and remains Standard Oil. The problem with this narrative is that the cost of supplying artificial light to a home or office fell steadily. Whale oil cost $3/gallon in 1858. By 1885, kerosene cost 8¢/gallon, and the cost of keeping a lamp lit was a cent per hour. Between 1880 and 1890, the output of petroleum products rose by 393 percent, and the price declined by 61 percent. Standard got 90 percent market share by improving efficiency and cutting price, not by being an exploitive monopolist.

So the fact is the opposite of the popular impression: from the consumers' point of view, Standard Oil was a paragon of public benefit. It took real PR talent on the part of the Progressives to turn it into the definitive symbol of abuse. In the end, as is true of any monopoly not enforced by government, its power was eroded by competitors as the gasoline age began, and the 1911 antitrust case breaking up the company was a pointless exercise.

For the most part, the antimonopoly movement was fueled by locally powerful businesses seeking legislation against the more efficient, large-scale entities that came into existence because of the increased efficiencies created by the nationwide scope of communications and transportation. Antitrust was, and remains, primarily a body of law used by vested interests to defend against the onslaughts of change.

The big businesses of the time should not be idealized, because many of them did hope to gain monopoly power and then raise prices. Their problem was that the strategy did not work. Few industries lend themselves to monopoly, as long as competitors are free to enter.

In the 1890s, the government attacked the cordage trust. Its operators wanted a monopoly, but the trust fell into a pattern of buying out manufacturers at a premium in the hope of obtaining monopoly power over prices, whereupon the sellers took the money and bought more rope-making machines, which they then used to undercut the trust's prices until the trust bought them out again. This was not a winning strategy for the trust.

Valid or not, the fear of market power was a powerful force for the expansion of activist government. If one accepted a need for government regulation to overtly correct the balance between such mighty forces as "labor" and "capital", or "farmers" and "railroads", then one was led logically to reject the third pillar of the Old Republic, that the government was not and need not be "in charge" and responsible. If government decided whose bargaining power needed to be shored up in the private sector, then it was "in charge", by definition, because it could easily determine the outcomes under the guise of equalizing the forces.

So the Progressive Movement of the turn of the century had two faces. On the one hand, it hewed to the Old Republic's fears of corruption and capture by faction, and advocated direct democracy, direct election of senators, and mechanisms such as the initiative, referendum, and recall of elected officials.

On the other, the Progressives rejected the tenet that the government was not responsible, and advocated more government power in almost every dimension. But this was to be a different kind of power—exercised by expert elites using commissions and agencies, shielded from corrupt legislators, and deriving political legitimacy from their expertise and (theoretical) lack of connection to affected interest groups.

There is an echo of the Great Chain of Being here, with the ruler legitimized by his superior wisdom and virtue. Of course, if one's legitimacy rests on superior wisdom and virtue, one must demonstrate these in practice.

The ICC model of the expert regulatory agency was replicated with the FDA in 1906, the FTC in 1914, and many public utility commissions in the states. The change was momentous, but before the Great Depression of the 1930s, the dragon of government by regulatory agencies exercising power delegated to them by legislatures was still in its egg.

Another baby dragon was also quiet—the income tax, which was made constitutional by the Sixteenth Amendment in 1916. Later, this became one of the great building blocks of Big SIS, because it produced revenues that could be handed out and opportunities for favors in the form of special tax breaks. The latter particularly lend themselves to systemic corruption because they are opaque. Only the IRS knows exactly how much an interest is harvesting.

The heyday of the model that experts should run the government came during World War I. The war justified deep intrusion into the national industrial machine and national life generally, including serious repression of dissent. The era also pioneered the creation of councils of representatives of private interests, which would coordinate the national effort. Such councils usually conclude that the national interest is congruent with the private interests of its members, so most efforts turn into special-interest capture on steroids. The World War I councils foreshadowed the National Recovery Administration of the New Deal that came fifteen years later,

The Old Republic as of 1929: battered but upright

Still, after World War I, the power of government retreated, and the assumptions of the Old Republic were in reasonable shape. The Progressive Movement had made mistakes in its excessive faith in government and experts, but its program had been largely motivated by the familiar concerns of the Old Republic—the fear of corruption and of special interests' capture of government—even if the application of these principles had gotten a bit skewed. So it was possible to return to the premises that no one was really in charge of society and the economy except God. Government had its proper functions, but it was not responsible for the overall design and performance of the civilization.

The ethos of the times met the definition of conservatism presented by Jonah Goldberg in *Liberal Fascism* as "opposed to all forms of political religion", a "rejection of the idea that politics can be redemptive", and "the conviction that a properly ordered republic has a government of limited ambition".

The election of 1920 endorsed this conservatism, as Warren Harding restated the old faith: "[N]o government is worthy of the name which is directed by influence on the one hand, or moved by intimidation on the other." He also promised a rest from the turmoil of the preceding twenty years of Progressivism and World War I: "America's present need is not heroics, but healing; not nostrums, but normalcy".

Granted, Harding's later decision to have sex with a mistress in a White House coat closet might cast a bit of doubt on his good judgment, but the man had solid political sense. (On the other hand, maybe he was just ahead of his time, as his sexual precedent was followed by FDR (maybe), JFK, LBJ, and WJC.) As a representative of the values of the Old Republic, Harding got 60 percent of the vote, against the Democrat's 34 percent. Socialist Eugene Debs got 3.4 percent, down from his 6 percent in 1912, but he had to run his campaign from the Atlanta Federal Penitentiary, where President Wilson had put him for opposing World War I. (Harding let him out.)

In 1921, in the aftermath of the postwar adjustment, the nation was hit with a severe depression, with unemployment jumping to 11.7 percent and the price index falling

15 percent. The government sprang into…non-action. It let events take their course, and the depression was sharp but short. By 1922, things started to roll again, and by 1923, unemployment was at 2.4 percent and the nation swung into that great exuberant era called "the 20s".

The Great Depression, the New Deal, and the onrush of Big SIS

The Great Depression of 1929 changed things. Whether it could have been shortened by the 1921 approach of non-action is a lively topic of discussion these days as people debate how to avoid the Depression of 2012, but this was not the course chosen. President Herbert Hoover was an engineer; engineers fix things that are broken, and he set out to fix the economy with relief programs, a 42 percent increase in federal spending, public works, financial backstops, defense of gold, and tariffs.

The activism did not work and may have made things worse. GDP went from $103.6 billion in 1929 (in current-at-the-time dollars) to $56.4 billion in 1933, and unemployment exceeded 25 percent. Prices fell by 24 percent.

When the New Deal came onstage, the retail principle applied—the government had helped break the economy, so now it owned it. The response to failed activism was more activism, as Roosevelt doubled down on all the anti-depression measures. During the 1932 campaign, Roosevelt excoriated Hoover's spending and promised a balanced budget, but these promises quickly disappeared.

FDR kept one campaign promise. Speaking at Oglethorpe University in May 1932, he said, "The country needs and, unless I mistake its temper, the country demands bold, persistent experimentation. It is common sense to take a method and try it: If it fails, admit it frankly and try another. But above all, try something."

This was the theme of the New Deal, except of course that there was no admission of any failures. The result was a series of *ad hoc* measures, untied to any theory of anything, and consisting mainly of shoring up special interests. In 1940, Alvin Hansen, a leading New Deal's economic advisor, was asked whether its basic economic principle was sound. He answered: "I really do not know what the basic principle of the New Deal is."

The first step was a necessary response to the banking panic of 1933. Banks were closed temporarily and audited, and only sound ones were allowed to reopen. The next step was to increase the price of gold, which most economists also applaud.

Actions on gold went further, though. In a sweeping *ipse dixit*, the government nullified both public and private promises to pay in gold. The action was a default on 43 percent of the national debt. It also gave haircuts to people who had received promises of payment in gold, and gave windfalls to their promisors, who could now repay in paper. The effect is with us still; a long-term renter under a pre-1933 contract with a gold clause pays about 4 percent of the fair rental.

The goal of farm policy became a return to "parity", defined as the ratio of farm to industrial prices that prevailed from 1910 to 1914. Considering the intervening technological and economic changes, this was absurd, but, as J. R. Dunn observes:

> For two years, in a country where hunger was a serious problem and starvation an actual possibility, the federal government at a cost of over $700 million plowed under fields of grain, slaughtered and condemned over 6 million pigs, and burned the entire southern cotton crop, sending masses of destitute blacks fleeing north in search of simple survival.

While the government was determined to raise farm prices as compared with the prices of other goods, another agency devoted itself to raising the prices of the other goods. The New Deal established the National Recovery Administration to turn the nation's economic system into a series of cartels.

A couple of years later, the government reversed itself, and the Department of Justice started suing large industries for price fixing, the very activity that the National Recovery Act had forced them to engage in under pain of criminal prosecution.

The Wagner Act increased the cost of labor at a time of high unemployment and shriveled investment. It also started a long, symbiotic relationship between urban political machines, selected unions, and organized crime, a devil's bargain that still haunts us.

The telephone and radio companies were given the Federal Communications Commission, which achieved an awesome record of capture by special interests and suppression of competition and innovation. As a snapshot of a big topic, consider that the FCC suppressed the deployment of the superior technology of FM radio for twenty-six years.

The trucking industry was brought under the ICC, both to protect railroads from competition and to keep the truckers from undercutting each other. The airline industry was made into a cartel. Social Security was started, as was a national welfare program.

The Wall Street financial community, blamed for the 1929 crash, was regulated. Perhaps the level of fraud decreased—as is true of late nineteenth-century history, the facts are hidden by a cloud of propaganda—but the price was high. In the 1920s, finance was slowly decentralizing away from New York and into the rest of the nation. The securities laws stopped this and gave Wall Street control of the capital markets right down to the present day. These laws also prevented new forms of financing and inhibited the flow of capital to innovators. This was eased somewhat in the 1980s, with the development of junk bond financing, but recent "reforms" are restoring the old status quo.

The banking industry received help in numerous ways, including a rule forbidding it to pay depositors any interest on demand deposits. Banks got to use savers' money for free.

The Federal Housing Administration was created, starting an eighty-year run of federal government subservience to an iron quadrangle of real estate developers, brokers, banks, and title insurers. The coalition was joined later by the antipoverty and antidiscrimination industries.

The courts resisted some of the New Deal measures and approved others. Constitutional scholar Barry Cushman makes a convincing case that the Supreme Court maintained its focus on the old standard of not allowing class legislation, but applied and adapted it to the new circumstances. He also analyzes polling data from the late 1930s that shows that American people as a whole still held the basic values of the Old Republic.

The judicial system could not check the tide of special-interest favoritism unaided, though, and it was reluctant to stand in the way of the experimental spirit. Eventually the defenses against Big SIS cracked. Then, because the New Deal had no guiding principles or theories, the government had no ready reason for rejecting anything proposed by the forces of faction and corruption beating on its doors.

The approach fostered government by freelancer. If underlying principle is lacking, anyone in an administration with an idea has a good shot at getting it enacted to law. Why not? One "experiment" is as good as another when one is acting at random. Then each failed experiment becomes a reason for yet more experiments, often directed at making up for the damage caused by the last one.

To maintain political legitimacy, though, activists needed to create a facade of knowledge. So the New Deal resurrected the Progressive-Era idea that government power was legitimized by superior expertise and used it to justify whatever bubbled to the top of the agenda.

The reality was far different, and New Dealer Raymond Moley wrote in 1940:

> To look upon these programs as the result of a unified plan was to believe that the accumulation of stuffed snakes, baseball pictures, school flags, old tennis shoes, carpenter's tools, geometry books, and chemistry sets in a boy's bedroom could have been put there by an interior decorator.

The activism was also supported by an unending tide of propaganda. As Jonah Goldberg documents in *Liberal Fascism*, Atlantic civilization of the 1930s was characterized by an odd and disturbing state-worship. In Europe, it led to Mussolini, Hitler, and Stalin, and whatever one thinks of FDR, it is on the plus side of his ledger that it did not happen here.

The state-worship was particularly unsettling in that none of the policies had any basis in a serious understanding of the economy and its maladies. Nor did they have any basis in political theory—except the Progressive idea that experts should be in charge, so shut up.

Conservatives say that the New Deal did not end the Depression, and from some perspectives they have a point. Unemployment remained high. In 1938, it was at 19 percent or 11 percent, depending on whether you count people on government-paid work relief as employed or unemployed. GDP was $91.9 billion in 1937, far below the $131 billion GDP it would have achieved had the economy grown at 3 percent per year from 1929 to 1927.

To the contemporaries, the New Deal looked better. A nasty recession occurred in 1938, but on the whole, whether because of its policies or in spite of them, the New Deal had the Mandate of Heaven on its side. The 1937 GDP was way below the possible trend line, but it was up 63 percent from its 1933 nadir and only 10 percent below that of 1929. Taking into account the 15 percent fall in the price index between 1929 and 1937, this felt like recovery. The stock market almost quadrupled between 1932 and 1937.

The late 1930s were a good time for the employed—*their* economy had come back a long way. It is hard to quarrel with success, and the New Deal looked pretty good, especially when judged in the context of the raw panic of early 1933.

In its 1937 term, the Supreme Court largely gave up trying to stem the tide of special interest laws and got out of the business of serious review of economic legislation. It never quite said, "Do whatever", but it adopted the "rational basis" test, which still prevails. As long as a legislature presents a good cover story on why a law regulating commerce, property, or economic affairs can be justified by a chain of logic that connects it to a legitimate government purpose, a court will not second-guess.

Important segments of the intellectual classes provided support for this deference, defending it not just in terms of the preeminence of the democratic will of the people but on the grounds that capture of the state by special interests is a virtue, not a flaw. The takeover was given a label— Interest Group Liberalism or Pluralist Democracy—and the clash of factions capturing government was somehow to produce beneficent policy.

The obvious analogy is to the invisible hand of the free market, which, in theory, produces beneficent outcomes in the economic sphere. Unfortunately, while the theory and limits of the free economic market have been well worked out and widely verified in practice, the analogy of an invisible-hand political marketplace has no such underpinnings. The idea that the collision of interest groups creates a political market that operates akin to the economic market was merely an arresting metaphor, not a theory, and it has not stood up well.

World War II diverted the nation's energy. In 1946, there was a brief return to normalcy, such as had happened after previous wars, and some rollback of labor's privileges. There was also the most-predicted depression that never happened. The New Dealers assumed that unemployment would return with a vengeance if demobilization proceeded rapidly, but they were dead wrong. The nation absorbed the returning vets, and a boom started.

The Cold War solidified governmental authority and responsibility, and national security was used as a justification for everything. Even the highway system was the National Defense Highway Act, and the space race became the justification for spending on education.

However, the changes that the New Deal made in the economy were not seriously challenged. The new structure probably retarded innovation and growth, but no one can prove it. In the 1950s, the nation accepted the idea of Big Government (with its bigness focused mainly on defense), Big Business, and Big Labor as the triumvirate of power.

It was not generally noted that during this era, the United States was luxuriating in the industrial dominance that followed the destruction of other industrial nations in World War II and that we embraced a system whereby the interests used the government to help them divide the monopoly profits that came from this dominance. Nor was it noted how much the nation relied on discrimination against minorities and women to staff crucial parts of the economy at bargain wages. Those lessons were waiting.

Big SIS triumphant: the Great Society and after

The next great wave in the creation of Big SIS came in the 1960s, with the Great Society and its 40-odd programs, including civil rights, Medicare, urban development, education, environmental law, labor matters, and even the arts, and its further expansion during the Nixon years.

Conservatives sometimes mumble darkly about the New Deal as a bunch of Commies imposing central planning on the economy. This was not totally wrong, but the griping was about thirty years premature.

The New Deal did indeed house many who dreamed of five-year plans and a native version of socialism. FDR's speech at Oglethorpe, famous now for the "bold experimentation" line, focused primarily on the need for thoroughgoing planning to prevent the waste of resources that, in his view, occurred in a free economy. This perspective was the opposite of the experimental mind-set that characterizes an entrepreneurial, free-market system. But in practice, the New Deal was characterized by the opposite of planning—it was a mad scramble for control of pieces of the government by assorted interests with little coordination and no consistency.

Nonetheless, the seed of the concept of rule by disinterested experts remained alive in political circles, and it blossomed in the 1960s. If the New Deal consisted of *ad hoc* responses to distressed interest groups, the Great Society was based on concepts of planned social systems on a large scale.

The New Deal regulated many existing industries or economic sectors, but it remained a regulator rather than a prime mover. The job of an FCC or an FDA was to respond to what private sector actors brought to it. Even the labor legislation creating the National Labor Relations Board put the government in the role of referee between the private actors of business and labor. The referee might punch one side or the other sometimes, but it was not a contestant.

The Great Society was different. The government assumed responsibility for important systems. It would create model cities. It took over the housing market. It minutely regulated the environment. It accepted far greater responsibility for the overall performance of the economy than ever before—"fine-tuning" was the mantra of the day. It promised to wipe out poverty. It started the large-scale support of rail mass transit and hoped to reverse the suburbanization of the nation. In the 1970s, the Great Society list of programs was augmented by Nixon's expansions of environmental and welfare programs, and then later by the addition of sweeping Clean Air Amendments and the Americans with Disabilities Act pushed by Bush I.

The Great Society laws were designed by mandarins to be administered by their own ilk, and the creation of such great responsibility dictated that the government must be granted the great power necessary to achieve the grand schemes.

In practice, Great Society government was a three-way internal contest. One group consisted of mandarins, such as me and my Bureau of the Budget/Executive Office of the President colleagues, who drank the old Progressive Kool-Aid of orderly government by rational and public-spirited experts, such as ourselves. Another was the Power-to-the-People crowd of the War on Poverty, which would morph into the '60s radicals and, ultimately, into the academic left and middle class rebels. The third was the congeries of interest groups created or reinforced by the New Deal, such as the housing, education, agriculture, transportation, and welfare industries, with a strong power base in every congressional district. They regarded the Great Society as the grandest pork barrel anyone could ever imagine and eyed the other contestants with disbelieving amusement that anyone could be so naïve.

Of course, the assertion that the government could accomplish any of its announced aims was presumptuous fantasy, especially when most of the supporting coalition, including Congress, regarded anything other than pork-barrel politics as a silly in-joke designed to fool the yokels. The special interests soon won the three-way tug of war, with the radicals left behind until they wised up and joined the interests, and the mandarins still milling around back at the starting gate.

While the grand purposes were never realistic, the power given the government because of the grandiosity of ambition remained. In the wake of the Great Society, all the restraints of the Old Republic were pretty much wiped out. Special-interest capture was accepted rather than abhorred, government responsibility for everything was both assumed and glorified, and systemic corruption became pandemic.

Completing the structure

The Great Society is not quite the end of the story of the creation of present-day Big SIS. Four more factors were necessary to complete the structure .

Two of these were substance: the Civil Rights Movement and environmentalism, which started as moral movements rather than self-interested ones and thus gathered immense momentum.

The third was structural—the creation of a network of regulatory agencies and the delegation of vast power to them. This trend started as far back as the ICC and accelerated during the New Deal, but it was during the 1960s and 1970s that the Regulatory State became the center of gravity of American government and a major enabler of Big SIS.

The fourth factor, also structural, was the reaction of private actors to the growth of big government. The rising tide of government money and power made it worthwhile for special interests to organize. They needed to defend what they had been given and work for more. These incentives triggered positive feedback; the bigger Big SIS became, the greater became the pressures to make it even bigger.

These factors are outlined *seriatum.*

Civil Rights

The Civil Rights Movement was a faction within the meaning of the Founders' definition, but it was not primarily an economic interest. It derived its political legitimacy and the power of its demands from an overwhelming moral claim on society.

Civil rights advocates were correct in asserting that meeting their demands was good for other interests and for society as a whole. Martin Luther King made this point eloquently when he said that the "disinherited children of God [who] sat down at lunch counters…were in reality standing up for the best in the American dream and the most sacred values in our Judeo-Christian heritage." But the general welfare argument was not really necessary to the movement's power.

A tragedy of U.S. history is that in 1861 the antislavery Republicans constituted only about half of the voters in the North. Many of the War Democrats would fight for the Union but not against slavery. Lincoln needed great political dexterity to keep the North harnessed and the war effort going.

The result was a near-run thing. Sherman took Atlanta shortly before the 1864 election, which made up for three years of grisly stalemate in the East. Had Sherman failed, the Democrats might well have won the election and made peace.

In 1864, desperate to keep the War Democrats on board, Lincoln ran on the Union ticket, not the Republican, and chose as his vice president Andrew Johnson, who served as war governor of his native Tennessee during its occupation by Union troops. Johnson had little use for the aristocratic planter class, but he preferred to let this class reclaim its old privileges if the alternative was political and economic equality for the freed slaves.

Johnson became president in April 1865. None of the 166 regiments of U.S.C.T. (United States Colored Troops) were invited to the Grand Review in Washington in May 1865, when 200,000 victorious Union soldiers marched past the nation's dignitaries. In the South, Johnson restored the planter hierarchy, giving back lands that Union generals had taken from rebels and redistributed to Freedmen.

When General Ulysses Grant became president in 1868, he acted strongly to put down the Ku Klux Klan and other White Terror, but the economic cast had been set, and the Radical Republicans ("Radical" meant "wanted racial justice"), Freedmen, and their southern dependents had no economic power base.

The moral crusade against slavery did not extend to embracing full equality, and the Radical Republicans lost their working majority in the country as a whole. Helped by a couple of distressing Supreme Court decisions, the "Redeemer" movement took back control of the old Confederacy, stripping the Freedmen of guns, votes, property, justice, and often life, as the North looked the other way.

Between 1882 and 1968, 3,241 African Americans and 552 Caucasians were lynched in the old Confederate/Border states, and this excludes the 1865–82 period, which saw a high level of Redeemer violence.

Occasional Republican efforts to enact anti-lynching laws were filibustered by the southern Democrats. African Americans were consigned to segregation and debt peonage for another ninety years.

The Founders' assumption that a minority would not tolerate such oppression from a majority did not come true, largely because the Redeemers pre-empted the Second Amendment and disarmed the Freedmen. Just as the almost 200,000 African Americans who had fought for the Union during the Civil War were not invited to the Grand Review in 1865, they did not attend the national festival of reconciliation held at Gettysburg in 1913, except as servants.

Some Radical Republicans thought, rightly, that the best solution after the Civil War would have been disenfranchisement of the ruling class of the Confederacy in addition to massive land confiscation and redistribution to both ex-slaves and poor whites, to give these antagonists a common stake in the new order. No one can prove whether this would have been successful, but the policy actually adopted did not work for either ex-slaves or ex-masters.

Much of the politics of the late nineteenth century was based on the failure of Reconstruction and the acceptance of its failure by the North. As long as northern interests did not interfere with the South's self-crippling obsession with racial inequality, they obtained great leeway to pursue internal improvements, the protective tariff, a stream of bountiful pensions to Civil War veterans, and protection of national commerce.

Historians attribute the stagnation of the post-Civil War South to many causes, including shortage of capital and poor infrastructure (which is much the same thing).

But capitalists in the nineteenth century went to the ends of the earth seeking profit, and it is hard to believe they could not find the old Confederacy. The more persuasive explanation is that the South adopted the *latifundio* mentality, where property rights and social structure were used to prevent development, which threatened the racial balance. It is a sobering lesson that societies can retrogress as well as progress, and that property rights can be harnessed to the cause of stasis as well as dynamism.

The situation began to change during World War I and then between the wars, as a million African Americans migrated to the North and West. Nonetheless, the basic bargain continued right up to the 1950s. Neither the Progressive Movement nor the New Deal was a friend of civil rights. Woodrow Wilson, elected in 1912, was horrified to find African Americans in the Federal Civil Service treated decently and set about to re-segregate it. He also loved the hideously racist movie, *Birth of a Nation.* (There is a good reason you no longer hear the Democratic Party talk about its Wilsonian heritage.)

In 1931, Congress passed the Davis-Bacon Law, which was designed to keep African Americans from working on federally financed construction projects. After Roosevelt's election, agricultural policy paid southern land owners for not growing cotton, but the money did not filter down to the sharecroppers, who migrated, pulled by the opportunities in industry and pushed by southern poverty. Industry in the North and West was not roses, though, in part because many unions were highly discriminatory, especially in the building trades. They were protected by their political ties to the Democratic Party.

When America's true morality finally reasserted itself, the obligation was heavy. Georges Clemenceau, the future premier of France during World War I, was a reporter in the United States during Reconstruction. In 1870, he said:

[W]ith the ratification of the Fifteenth Amendment, the American revolution is over. . . The rash violation of justice which unleashed it has been both punished and expiated. For to the glory of human nature be it said that, as long as justice is disregarded, the avenging spirit lives on, and there can be only one way of ending all questions: that is to solve them in accordance with justice.

Clemenceau was woefully premature, because the completion of the revolution of the Civil War had to await the post-World War II Civil Rights Movement.

The political conflict is still with us. Moral claims do not come with sharp definitions, and much of U.S. politics for the past half century has revolved around the boundaries. Were the moral claims met when legal discrimination was ended? Legal and private discrimination? When the effects of past discrimination were neutralized—if they were— and when was that? To what degree must basic structures of society be changed to overcome the results of past evil?

Other groups also recognized that moral claims are powerful, and they made their own. After a time, moral claims were made by everyone except straight, nondisabled Caucasian males. (And we're working on it—after all, many ethnic males were subject to great discrimination.)

Many of these moral claims were valid, but, especially as time has passed and discrimination has been corrected, mixed in with the genuine claims is considerable opportunism and posturing. No representatives of any group are paid to be reasonable. They see their job as ensuring that no progress is regarded as sufficient, and that opposition to any demand should be treated as a hate crime and put beyond the pale of public discussion. This stance is also much in the personal interests of the representatives, who have no interest in seeking other lines of work.

Much of the current debate over "the welfare state" is actually a continuation of the debate over the nature and limits of the old obligation identified by Clemenceau "to solve [all questions] in accordance with justice."

Environmentalism

The other great moral movement was environmentalism.

To most of us, environmental protection is primarily a pragmatic issue. We believe in conservation, as in parks, open spaces, and undeveloped areas. We like clean air and water, and we like nature. We want to see the environment protected.

A society on the edge of existence does not worry about proper disposal of mining slag or a bit of air and water pollution, and does not hesitate to clear-cut a forest if necessary to make room for crops. As our society has grown richer, it has come to value environmental amenities more and pollution-producing goods less, so it is only natural that protecting the environment has moved up the priority list. Wealth creates more choices. Therefore, we conclude, by all means let us continue to get richer so we can afford even more environmental protection.

In this rationalist calculus, environmental protection presents four kinds of issues:

- Preventing the use of air, water, and land as a waste dump, and trading off the costs of emissions control against the need for economic activity and personal freedom (as in auto-mobility), as emissions can rarely be held to zero. While society has a rich history of nuisance law on environmental issues, the doctrines did not keep up with the evolving views of the community and often failed to deal with pollution when transaction costs are high. People grew impatient waiting for the nuisance law system to develop solutions, and demanded government actions. There is an echo of the urban waste issue of the nineteenth century.

- Providing public goods, such as parks and views, and protecting animal species that we like (grizzly bears), and cleaning up past contamination.

- Classic problems of "the commons", when a lack of property rights in a resource provides incentives for its overuse and exhaustion. Pastures and fishing areas are good examples.

- Government subsidies and other incentives for environmental destruction, as mentioned in the tale of the barrier islands in chapter 1. Much of the dam building of the twentieth century made little sense in terms of economics and was the product of special-interest pressure.

True Green environmentalists see it quite differently. To them, the cause is a moral imperative, independent of costs and benefits. Indeed, True Greens seem happiest when the costs of protection or cleanup are high. To someone who regards pollution as a sin, these costs are a proper expiation; high costs mean that the sin was grievous indeed.

As Ted Nordhaus and Michal Schellenberg, environmental strategists and founders of the Breakthrough Insitute, observed:

[Rachel Carson's] *Silent Spring* [in 1962] set the template for nearly half a century of environmental writing: wrap the latest scientific research about an ecological calamity in a tragic narrative that conjures nostalgia for Nature while prophesying ever worse disasters to come, unless human societies repent their sins against Nature and work for a return to a harmonious relationship with the natural world.

The difference in these perceptions has created a strange politics. The Carson approach has generated a strong level of fuzzy public support at the general level, especially because the public has remained unaware that her "science" was extremely dubious. But the public also assumes that the movement has a decent regard for pragmatic compromise between environmental and economic needs.

In reality, environmental protection policy is run by the True Greens, who have formed an alliance with assorted corporate crony capitalists, legal entrepreneurs, academic grantsmen, and anti-industrial activists. Combined, they have captured policy-making instruments in the federal government.

The only pragmatism about current environmental policy is the determination whether a particular policy pushes beyond political limits. Of economic and social rationality, there is little.

The Regulatory State

The third development essential to Big SIS is the multiplication of powerful regulatory agencies. The Regulatory State is an essential building block of the Special Interest State.

Before the explosion of regulatory agencies, national policy was mostly debated in Congress. Internal improvements or tariffs or disaster relief might be contentious, but questions were resolved in the open forum of congressional politics. Elections were fought out over the parties' different views.

The Interstate Commerce Commission (ICC) and then the Sherman Act were the first great federal delegations of regulatory power to subordinate units. With the ICC, the delegation was explicit—"deal with the railroad issue". The Sherman Act was tacit. The statute forbade all combinations in restraint of trade, a command that, taken literally, would abolish contracts. So the courts created and administered an antitrust regulatory regime, which was endorsed by Congress in later laws and then augmented by the creation of the Federal Trade Commission in 1914.

The states followed suit, with their own regulatory commissions to govern network industries of all kinds.

When the tide of lawmaking rose in the 1930s, there came a dilemma. Inherent in the expansion of governmental power was the complicated question of how this unbridled power would be exercised. As the reach of any institution expands, especially anything as cumbersome as a government, it becomes impossible for the institution as a whole to exercise its power. Delegation to subunits is necessary: to agencies, legislative committees, even private groups.

Congress itself fragmented into a multitude of committees and subcommittees, each with life-or-death power over some piece of the federal bureaucracy. Committee responsibilities were further divided between substantive law and budgetary appropriations.

Congress also enacted general laws delegating power to regulatory agencies. Because Congress was active in so many areas, the number of agencies multiplied, and the authority given existing cabinet departments multiplied as well. All were given power to make and enforce the rules within their areas of authority.

The great subsidy programs of the 1960s, such as health and education, triggered the creation of more regulatory empires because subsidies require rules to determine who is eligible and who is not, and to settle disputes. The contemporary health care industry revolves around HHS regulations.

Lyndon Johnson's Great Society of the 1960s was only part of the story; it created the education, civil rights, and health empires. But it was Richard Nixon who added, or allowed Congress to add, another wave of regulatory empires—the Environmental Protection Agency, the Occupational Health and Safety Administration, the Equal Employment Opportunities Commission, and the Endangered Species Act. Bush I added to the regulatory domain with the Americans with Disabilities Act and the Clean Air Amendments of 1990.

All these regulatory empires started with the proposition that the government was assuming primary and plenary responsibility for some area of national life. In theory, Congress could do the job of exercising the responsibility itself, but considering all the other areas of national life that need controlling, this is not practical.

So congressional practice is to enact a broad statute delegating great power to an agency. Much of the delegation is vague because Congress made no decisions as to the policy to be followed; that is left up to the agency. When a statute is specific, the detail is often there only because interest groups have managed to get pet language inserted in the statute. Even within a single regulatory system, the overall structure may lack consistency, clarity, and coherence, and of course the potential for conflict among the different regulatory empires is mind-bending.

One common fight during a legislative process is over the degree to which an agency should consider values other than the ones that it was created to protect. When OSHA issues a workplace safety standard, for example, is it required, or even allowed, to consider whether employers can meet the standard without going out of business? Should establishing an air quality target take into account the costs of meeting it? Congress often weasels on such issues, leaving the final decision to the courts.

To some extent, the underlying theory behind these broad delegations is the old Progressive Era idea that an expert agency, insulated from politics, should decide important questions. But the idea that agencies with immense power to do people good or harm could remain immune to political pressure was always absurd and has grown more so with the passing years, as interests have learned how to organize, the better to apply pressure on the agency, the public, and the Congress.

The consequence is special-interest capture on steroids. Control is given to those with the greatest ideological interest or the most money at stake.

The government has been parceled out. The Department of Labor and the National Labor Relations Board largely serve unions. The Environmental Protection Agency is the province of the True Greens. The Department of Energy is usually the servant of the big energy companies, but that is changing under current White House pressure to make it a slush fund for alternative energy sources. Health and Human Services is a cockpit for the struggles of various segments of the health care industry. The Federal Communications Commission was the abject servant of the broadcast and telecom industries for decades, but now it more often answers to an amorphous collection of self-proclaimed "public interest" groups, except insofar as its freedom is limited by the reality that the telecommunications system must actually allow communication, and that the powerful technology industries must be able to sell their toys.

Treasury and the Federal Reserve Board belong to the banks. The Securities and Exchange Commission serves mostly as a cartel for the securities industry, ensuring that minor frauds do not taint the industry while guarding against serious challenges to the status quo. Housing and Urban Development is a subsidiary of its client groups in housing and finance.

This whole regulatory structure is replicated at the state level, where dozens of powerful agencies have been created, each with its constituency.

Capture of these agencies is inevitable. The statutes are complex, and so are the technical dimensions of many of the issues. Only someone with a large economic or ideological stake can afford the investment of time and money necessary to understand the issues, to keep track of developments and analyze proposals, and to gin up support or opposition.

The public is rationally ignorant. Who in his right mind would make a hobby of understanding solid waste regulation, for example? Yet if you do not do it full time, you cannot be adequately informed.

The courts occasionally intervene, as they are charged with reviewing agency actions to make sure they comply with the law, but the presumption in favor of an agency is strong. Besides, the agency controls the technicalities, such as economic studies and risk assessments, and courts do not want to venture into these bogs.

Agencies are also dependent on Congress for money, people, and power. More specifically, they depend on the chairs of their particular committees. If the interests are dissatisfied with the agency, they can appeal to the Hill, hopefully with a better result. In *Government's End*, Jonathan Rauch vividly describes the fate of reformers who cross a special interest—not just a *powerful* interest, but *any* interest, right down to the mohair subsidy.

Positive feedback

A thermostat is a feedback mechanism. The temperature of the room rises, which triggers a switch, which sends a signal to the heater to shut down for a while. This is negative feedback, feedback that tamps down a cycle and keeps it in balance.

There is also positive feedback. It reinforces a cycle, as if a rise in temperature caused the thermostat to signal the furnace to increase its heat output rather than decrease it.

Big SIS is subject to positive feedback. Each increase in special-interest influence signals to other interests that they had better organize and get in the game, if they are not there already, or increase their efforts if they are.

Once, I asked a partner in a big Washington law firm whether he was worried by a nasty newspaper exposé of the undue power and influence wielded by his firm. "I am", he said. "I'm not sure we have enough people to handle all the business this is going to bring in."

As Big SIS has grown, so has the influence industry. The website *Open Secrets* shows 12,193 registered individual lobbyists dealing with Congress as of 2011, down from a high of 14,869 in 2007, and up from 10,406 in 1998.

The number of associations of all kinds has grown like kudzu. Reasons other than lobbying exist, of course, but lobbying is a powerful spark to their creation. Once an association exists, it inevitably becomes a lobbying group if some government action touches its interests, and, given the flood of actions, perceived impingements are as certain as death and taxes.

In the late 1920s, 400 lobbies were in the Washington telephone book. By 1950, there were 2000. The 2011 edition of the *Encyclopedia of Associations* claims there are 24,107 nonprofit organizations in the U.S. Not all of these engage in lobbying—included are athletic groups and fan clubs—but thousands do.

Jonathan Rauch documented the explosion in group membership following the Great Society. The AARP was founded in 1958, but its membership went from one to ten million between 1970 and 1980, then boomed to thirty-four million by 1990. It remains around thirty-five million in 2011. Membership in the American Federation of State, County, and Municipal Employees (AFSCM) went from 100,000 in 1955 to 1.3 million in 1998 and 1.6 million in 2011.

The Natural Resources Defense Council (NRDC), founded in 1970, has 1.3 million members, and the National Wildlife Federation has 4 million. The National Association of Home Builders went from 50,000 in 1967 to almost 200,000 in 1997.

As Rauch said:

Americans have no handle on the cannibalistic forces unleashed.…we created a government with vast power to reassign resources,…we created countless new groups. What we did not create... was a way to control the chain reaction set off when activist government and proliferating groups began interacting with each other.

Conservative blogger Glenn Reynolds put it succinctly: "With it raining federal soup, it is no surprise that interest groups have rushed out with buckets."

Furthermore, the explosion of programs increases the opportunities for that special type of log-rolling called "Bootleggers and Baptists". The term was coined by economist Bruce Yandle to describe alliances between interest groups with opposed values but with a common interest in a particular law. For example, state laws against selling alcohol were supported by both Baptists, who opposed alcohol use, and bootleggers, who profited from selling illegal alcohol once the legal sale was banned.

The bootlegger/Baptist combo couples ideological passions with financial motivations and resources, and the phenomenon has grown into a major dynamo of Big SIS. A common form now is the alliance of True Greens with businesses that will profit from green energy to support mandates and subsidies supporting ethanol, wind, and other alternatives to fossil fuel.

Tom Paine, where are you?

The next chapter explores the results of this history and the nuts and bolts of Big SIS—the subsidies, tax breaks, transfers, regulations, taxes, and laws.

But this chapter needs to end with a more general point: The United States no longer has a constitution in the small "c" sense. It has no "reasonably stable set of institutions through which a nation's fundamental decisions are made over a sustained period, and the principles that guide those decisions", to return to the earlier definition of "constitutional order".

The institutions may appear stable, but they are the subject of increasing scorn, attack, and disapproval. The principles that guide decisions are nonexistent. Claims of political legitimacy rest on shifting (and shifty, and shiftless) assertions of superior expertise, moral primacy, status as victim, log-rolling, control of powerful agencies, or tricky use of arcane Senate procedure or musty legal precedent. Whatever comes to the hand of a special interest is thrown into the battle.

Such claims lack tensile strength. We have no agreed-upon political theory that would define what governments should and should not do. Indeed, too many of us lack even the basic concept that there must be underlying and generally accepted principles of political legitimacy if our governments are to claim obedience and loyalty.

The Divine Right of Kings wore thin by 1776, when Thomas Paine wrote *Common Sense*. As of 2012, the Divine Right of Big SIS is also wearing thin. To adapt Paine's spoof of Divine Right to the modern age: "A bunch of special interests landing with an army of lawyers and establishing themselves as rulers of America, is in plain terms a very paltry rascally original. It certainly hath no divinity in it."

Chapter Three

Where We Are: Big SIS Today

Mapping the territory

To appreciate how pervasive and corrupt Big SIS has become, we can examine our current situation from three angles.

The first focuses on the old adage, "follow the money". U.S. Gross Domestic Product (GDP) in 2010 was $14.5 trillion. How much of this was spent directly by governments or according to their dictates? And how much of the governments' cut was bespoke by special interests rather than devoted to the general welfare and the basic functions of government?

The second perspective considers the effect of Big SIS on other essential institutions of our society. Even when governments are not directly allocating resources, how are incentives of private institutions skewed and their resources misdirected by governments' embrace of special-interest pleading?

The third angle is anecdotal. Historian Crane Brinton's classic *The Anatomy of Revolution* says that a harbinger of political upheaval is a feeling among important groups that "their opportunities for getting on in this world are unduly limited by political arrangements". They feel not simply "cramped" but "wronged", in ways that make them question the legitimacy of the existing order.

So this third section provides stories about government actions that arouse resentment, that make people feel both cramped and wronged, and that make the Saxon in his furrow say "This isn't fair dealing".

You can object to a list of horror stories on the ground that "data" is not the plural of "anecdote" and that a few stories do not necessarily represent the whole picture. True enough. On the other hand, the anecdotes keep piling up, and every day's batch of news clips provides a bounty of new outrages by Big SIS. Given enough of them, the plural of anecdote is indeed "information", even if it is not data that you can run through a computer. The unending stream of stories about stupid government tricks tells you that something is seriously amiss. Most importantly, it tells you that the legitimacy of the political order is fraying.

Following the money

Federal, state, and local governments levy against our national pot of a $14.5-trillion GDP (as of 2010) in five ways, taking money for themselves or shifting it around among private clients:

- Direct expenditures paid for by taxes and borrowing;

- Tax expenditures (special tax breaks) and collection costs;

- Loans, guarantees, and manipulation of interest rates;

- Regulatory requirements;

- Laws.

Direct expenditures

This is the biggest category of government impact. In January 2011, the Congressional Budget Office (CBO) projected 2011 federal spending as $3.7 trillion, almost 25 percent of GDP. State and local governments were on track to spend an additional $2.4 trillion, or 16 percent of GDP, for a total government take of 41 percent.

About 40 million people are employed by federal, state, and local governments, either directly or by contracted services. This is 26 percent of the U.S. labor force.

The federal government's activities include 2,001 separate subsidy programs, including 1,122 programs of aid to state and local governments. The total cost of all subsidies is hard to track, but outlays for the aid-to-governments category alone are $654 billion.

Tax expenditures (special tax breaks) and collection costs

"Tax expenditures" is the name budget analysts give to money not collected through the income tax system because Congress has granted a dispensation from the general rules. For 2011, these will reach $1.1 trillion.

The total income taxes collected from individuals and businesses will be $1.15 trillion, so the breaks are almost equal to the collections.

The exemption from taxes for employer-paid health insurance is a big item, at $160 billion, equaled by a variety of benefits for homeowners, and followed by the $120 billion in untaxed contributions to retirement plans. Many business interests get special tax breaks, but these tend to be small by government standards—chipping off a mere few tens of millions at a whack. They are a pervasive source of corruption, however, because they juice the Washington influence-peddling business, and the politicians expect *quid pro quos* from the recipients in the form of campaign contributions, jobs for staffers, and other coin.

The hideous complexity of the tax system also imposes huge compliance burdens, which must be included in an assessment of its costs. The CCH *Federal Tax Reporter* contains 72,536 pages of laws, rules, and rulings, and the office of the National Taxpayer Advocate estimates that taxpayers spend 6.1 billion hours on compliance. Economist Art Laffer builds on this number to estimate that compliance costs equal $431 billion annually, which means the costs of collection equal 30 percent of the taxes collected from individuals and businesses.

In terms of time, tax compliance eats up the equivalent of 2.5 percent of the nation's available work time. The arithmetic is that 6.1 billion hours equals 3.4 million work years, and the U.S. workforce is 140 million people.

Loans, guarantees, and manipulation of interest rates

As of 2008, the federal government had outstanding guarantees of $25 trillion, covering 59 percent of the total liabilities of financial firms. This included deposit insurance, the Freddie and Fannie guarantees, and pension benefits.

The annual value of these backstops, in terms of the insurance premium that the institutions should be paying to the taxpayers, is about $300 billion.

The Federal Reserve's low-interest-rate policies are not a loan guarantee, but some experts think they are in effect a tax on savers. The amount is $350 billion per annum, also for the benefit of financial institutions.

Financial firms are the big winners in this category, but many other interests also receive loans and guarantees. Student loan debt alone has reached $1 trillion outstanding, and the students are increasingly disinclined to repay it. A tour of the Catalogue of Federal Domestic Assistance turns up 130 different loan programs, including small business loans ($70 billion) and rural home loans ($16.2 billion). States have their own systems of loans and guarantees, of unknown dimension because but no one adds them all up.

Regulatory costs

The number of federal government agencies is countless, literally. The official list at *USA.gov* contains 479 distinct departments and agencies, but no standard exists for classifying parents and subunits and sub-subunits and so on. In the *Government Manual*'s index of agencies that appear in *Code of Federal Regulations*, the Department of Agriculture alone lists thirty-two distinct regulation-issuing subunits.

Clearly, hundreds of federal agencies have the power to issue regulations having the force of law. States and munic-ipalities echo the federal structure, with California alone listing over 500 agencies that employ more than 350,000 people. Add in all the states and cities and the number of rule-making entities mounts into the thousands.

The feds alone have imposed nearly 38,700 rules since 2001, including 3,573 in 2010, and the government's December 2010 *Regulatory Agenda* listed 4,225 pending regulatory actions, of which 224 would have an economic impact of $100 million or more. Congress passed 217 bills in 2010, so lawmaking is now more than 90 percent in the hands of agencies. The Big Five—Treasury, EPA, Commerce, HHS, and Agriculture—account for 43 percent of this.

The Competitive Enterprise Institute's annual publication *Ten Thousand Commandments* is the most comprehensive analysis of the costs of regulation. It puts these at about $1.8 trillion, as of 2008. I know of no estimate of regulatory compliance costs at the state and local level.

As government budgets grow tighter, the incentives grow for politicians to placate special interests by giving them control over regulatory processes. The result is disastrous. When a faction is looting the treasury, the cost is determinable, and the budget process imposes some limit, if only because other looters want to be sure that some funds are left for them. When a faction is imposing burdens on others or on the society as a whole through regulations, the costs are usually unknown, there is no limit, and other looters may not even realize that they are in a competition for resources.

Indeed, rather than compete, the potential beneficiaries of regulation are likely to log-roll, with each faction supporting all of the others' claims on the unlucky targets of the regulatory process.

A major paradox of contemporary government is that the rising concern about government expenditures contributes to the explosion in the volume and cost of regulation, as the factions shift their focus away from the budget and toward softer regulatory targets.

Laws

The estimates of regulatory costs presented in works such as *Ten Thousand Commandments* are based on the actions of administrative agencies that exercise power delegated to them by legislatures.

A separate legal domain is administered by judges through the court system, and no one tries to estimate its impacts on overall national resource allocation. The unspoken assumption is that all laws are *pro bono publico*, but this is obvious nonsense. Factions are very good at getting laws passed at all levels to promote their particular interests.

An analysis of the legal landscape should start with criminal laws, but the effort meets a couple of immediate roadblocks. First, it is genuinely hard to divide laws along the lines of special interest versus public benefit, even harder than for expenditures and regulations. Second, no one knows even the elementary fact of how many criminal laws the federal government has on the books, and states and cities add more layers of opacity.

For the feds alone, the total number of criminal laws is over 4,500, but they are scattered through so many provisions of the *United States Code* that a precise count is impossible. Nor does anyone even try to evaluate their impact. Common sense says the effect is large because the laws are numerous and often vague, the penalties fierce, and the costs of defense ruinous.

Also, the level of uncontrolled prosecutorial discretion is sobering. Everyone violates laws all the time—it is impossible to live without doing so—and whether any given citizen is put in jail is pretty much up to the prosecutors. This creates high payoffs for any special interest that captures a prosecutor's office. The ability to immunize your own team while criminalizing your opponents is valuable indeed.

Anyone who does not believe that such capture happens is naïve. The classic example, repeated many times in our history, is the alliance between police and prosecutors and a particular criminal gang that controls gambling, drugs, prostitution, and, in the 1920s Prohibition Era, booze. In this bargain, the state enforces the gang's monopoly by busting rivals in exchange for a cut of the loot, a lid on violence, and an operation kept in a low-enough key to avoid offending the middle class. (As a system, this arrangement can hold benefits for all, which is a reason it for its recurrence.)

More recently, *PJ Media* examined the resumes of 113 lawyers hired for the Civil Rights Division in the U.S. Department of Justice (DOJ). All, the study found, had histories of working for leftist groups that are eager to use the power of the government to push an aggressive agenda of "racial, gender, disability, and even sexuality preferences".

Also recently, a release of e-mails among climate change researchers showed a high level of mendacity and downright fraud, including participation by government agencies. DOJ is responding by seizing the computers and harassing bloggers who recycled the e-mails, but it is not investigating whether the authors of the e-mails participated in a scheme to defraud the government by falsifying research results. This demonstrates an interesting set of prosecutorial priorities.

Most recently, the Internet is alive with the observation that Martha Stewart went to jail as a result of a convoluted charge that she fibbed to the feds when she claimed she was innocent of insider trading, while political insider Jon Corzine disappeared over $1 billion of client money without, at least so far, any adverse personal consequence. Again, this provides an interesting window into federal prosecutorial choices.

Crony law also characterizes the civil justice system. An unholy alliance of elected state judges, the plaintiffs' tort bar, and the state attorneys general has been a blot on the law for decades, and a study by the Manhattan Institute concluded the following: "Few realize…just how in bed the litigation industry is with the very officials we entrust to enforce the law itself."

Antitrust law has little to do with protecting competition and much to do with protecting the income of the economists and lawyers who operate the system as well as the special interests that use these laws to suppress competition. As I wrote a decade ago: "When you have a century of experience with a program and virtually every landmark case looks to have been a mistake, perhaps it is time to stop saying, 'well, we'll get it right next time,' and start rethinking the basic premises."

Overall, the monetary impact of "The Law" is immense, but it is too large and foggy a territory to explore in depth here. It is a logical target for special-interest capture precisely because the costs are diffuse and hidden. For distressing detail, see *Overlawered.com*, which, as it describes itself, "explores an American legal system that too often turns litigation into a weapon against guilty and innocent alike, erodes individual responsibility, rewards sharp practice, enriches its participants at the public's expense, and resists even modest efforts at reform and accountability." If *Overlawyered* does not leave you catatonic with depression, then pick up Harvey Silverglate's *Three Felonies A Day: How the Feds Target the Innocent.*

Laws that facilitate the workings of the free economy and civil society, and that promote the classic function of allowing groups of cantankerous citizens to live together in peace and productivity, are a noble pillar of civilization. A legal system controlled by the shifting winds of special-interest capture is a road to delegitimizing a government.

And, as is true for the regulatory system, when political pressures impose limits on direct government expenditures, the focus of greedy factions turns to new laws, since these need not go through any rational review process whatsoever. If the burdens are sufficiently diffuse, and the identity of the true payers sufficiently obscure, then huge costs can be imposed for the sake of minor or purely symbolic benefits, and with little risk of electoral punishment.

Adding it up

No magic formula can tell us which government claims on resources support classic governmental functions or promote the general welfare, which benefit special interests, and which are pure waste.

In opinion polls, the general public usually says that about 40 percent of the federal budget is wasted, and this may be an example of the wisdom of crowds. Without breaking a sweat, the Cato Institute's *Downsizing Government* project identified $602 billion in budget cuts just from eight of the big cabinet departments, without even getting to Defense, Homeland Security, or Interior.

Estimates of waste are complicated because even worthy government programs mix private with public benefit. Late one evening several decades ago, my boss in the U.S. Bureau of the Budget looked up wearily from a stack of agency submissions and said:

> Government agencies have an interesting biology. Every program consists of a hard core of fat, surrounded by muscle and then with the bone on the outside. They say 'you're cutting to the bone!' and they're right—but that's because they won't let you get anywhere near the fat.

While some special-interest money is easy to identify—the 2000-plus subsidy programs, for example—much special-interest benefit is woven into the warp and woof of the programs.

The government subsidizes unions and their members by using above-market pay scales for government construction, but the amount of the subsidy is buried in a thousand different accounts. Education is an important function of governments, but a Heritage Foundation study of public school teacher salaries says they are about 50 percent above market rates—a transfer of $120 billion per year from taxpayers.

Special-interest influence grows as actions become less visible. It takes a really big interest, such as the elderly and their kin, to get something like Medicare through. As the price tag gets smaller, narrower interests have a chance, as in the $8 billion Universal Service Fund that subsidizes telecom connectivity and high tech equipment for schools and libraries. (Don't let anyone tell you that Silicon Valley is above participating in grubby Washington politics; when the dinner bell rings, it salivates.)

The ecosystem of Washington lobbying has niches for firms that specialize in helping clients bring home pork of particular kinds, such as programs to help local governments or educational institutions. The regulatory system, with its thousands of proceedings, murky costs, and speculative benefits, is also a good swamp for breeding virulent special-interest life forms. The climate change scare is creating a bonanza for influence peddlers and their clients, as ten big lobbying firms, "all with deep ties to Capitol Hill", represent over one hundred corporate clients hoping to batten on legislation mandating a cap-and-trade system to control carbon dioxide.

Many of the biggest-ticket items are environmental rules. EPA justly protests that forcing someone to stop dumping his waste into the water or air should not count as a "cost". If I keep my neighbor from dumping his garbage on my lawn, I am "imposing costs" on him, in a way, but society is all the better for it. People value the environment and are willing to pay to protect it, so EPA can fairly claim that many of the costs it imposes are justified.

On the other hand, the EPA skeptics (of which I am one), say that most of the low-hanging environmental-benefits fruit was picked decades ago. EPA justifies its current activism with a lot of dubious benefits analysis, and many of its rules are mostly cost with little benefit, dictated by a strange anti-industrial agenda of upper-class True Greens. Many of these are like the South Americans who enjoy living on *latifundios* with lots of peasants around, and so oppose economic development precisely *because* it would help the masses. They then ally with selected crony capitalist interests in a powerful bootleggers-and-Baptists coalition.

Whenever there is a danger that EPA or its True Green clients might be forced to admit that huge environmental progress has been made in some area, such as clean air, the agency makes the standard more stringent. This triggers new headlines about how many geographic areas are "not in attainment", ignoring the fact that they *were* in attainment before the change. The agency then uses the "non-attainment" as a reason beat the drums of "crisis", and to demand authority to impose ever-more-demanding rules. The current EPA leadership is constantly engaged in the move-the-goalpost game.

The size of the special interest state is also cloaked because the real parties in interest are often a couple of steps removed from easy visibility.

The tax deduction for home mortgage interest payments is defended by the web of housing interests that profit from a brisk market as much as by the homeowners themselves.

The deduction for retirement savings came with a stiff special-interest price. These savings must be channeled through the financial industry, which levies a toll of about 3 percent annually, a total of $90 billion in 2008, from direct fees and commissions derived from swapping stocks with each other. Other special interests also surround this deduction. You can dip into your account to buy a home (housing interests again), or buy education (academia), or for medical expenses (hospitals want to get paid), plus a catch-all for "severe financial hardship". Taking the money for anything else, such as starting a business, triggers hefty penalties.

In considering Big SIS, you must also face up to Social Security and Medicare.

I am sorry to say it, my fellow geezers (or should I say "senior Americans who have earned the respect of a grateful republic"?), but we are a special interest, and a huge one. As the blog *Powerline* put it:

> What is the central purpose of government? That question might be tricky to answer in theory, but here in the U.S., the practical answer is easy: the principal function of our national government is to transfer wealth from the young and the middle-aged to the elderly.

It went on to note that these transfers account for around $1.16 trillion, almost double the defense budget.

We seniors don't regard ourselves as a special interest because for seventy-five years the government has sold social security as a savings and insurance scheme whereby seniors finance their own retirement. But it is not so; the money flows out immediately.

Past retirees did very well; the base of workers expanded, and Congress kept upping the benefits. My generation is doing reasonably well in terms of getting back the money paid, plus some return. Future retirees will get hosed, because their money will have been paid to me, and not enough will come in to finance the Boomers. The economics of Medicare are even worse.

*   *   *   *

The bottom line from this survey of government expenditures, tax breaks, regulations, and laws is that distinguishing the programs that support the general welfare and public good from those based on special interest favoritism cannot be done with any precision. However, it is pretty clear that the special interest share is immense, and growing.

The examination also leads to an interesting conclusion about contemporary political debates. These often revolve around whether the United States should be a "welfare state", in which the people, acting through their representatives, direct their governments to perform many functions presumed to promote the general welfare or provide a safety net for the misfortunate. The position of the proponents is that opposing these enterprises shows that one is a selfish Scrooge.

The people of the United States are indeed generous, and want to provide safety nets to ensure that no one falls completely through the cracks, and to protect themselves and others from the blows of bad luck. This desire leads logically to the concept of the "welfare state", but that term is actually a long way from reality. "Special interest state" is more accurate because concern for either the neediest or the general welfare accounts for only a small portion of the expenditures and other resource transfers. Perhaps the greatest triumph of the massed factions that benefit from Big SIS is their success in hijacking the term "welfare state" to describe their collective greed.

Distorting other institutions

The basic numbers on the resources absorbed and allocated by governments are sobering.

But wait! There's more! as the infomercial guys say.

The leverage exerted by Big SIS affects decisions far beyond the money that it commandeers directly. It distorts the incentive structures throughout society and sends investors and workers skittering off in unproductive directions.

In *Government's End* (2000), Jonathan Rauch said that most estimates of the drain on the national economy from special-interest-caused distortions ranged between 5 and 12 percent of GDP. It certainly has not gone down in the past decade.

Housing is a huge example. The iron alliance of builders, developers, banks, title insurers, congressional committees, and government agencies has skewed national policy toward channeling savings into home building. In the 1990s, they were joined by the poverty warriors, who saw the middle class making money from rising home prices and thought that the poor should be cut in on the deal.

Homes are a strange kind of capital good, and, without government distortions to ensure continuing inflation, they are not a particularly suitable vehicle for personal savings. Most Americans are too reliant on the equity in their homes to finance retirement, and the risk grows for those farther down the economic ladder.

In 2008, we began reaping the harvest of this irrational, special-interest-driven government policy. Instead of learning the lesson, though, the government and its housing industry clients (or perhaps it is the housing industry and its government clients) seem determined to bring back the old days as quickly as possible by keeping interest rates low and using government guarantees to subsidize mortgages.

The tax law provision exempting employer-paid health insurance premiums from taxable income has been a disaster. It yokes health insurance to employment, which decreases labor mobility, skews pay systems, and distorts the health care industry and the insurance market.

Academia, a major client of Big SIS, is much in the news now, with arguments over whether a higher-education bubble exists. It does, as federal subsidies misdirect students into borrowing to buy expensive degrees that will not produce income for them. Student loan debt now exceeds $1 trillion, and this is only a small part of the total amounts that students have paid out over the past decades.

The availability of the subsidies has also allowed universities to raise their prices steadily, with themselves rather than the students reaping the benefits. Not only is much of the faculty doing very well, but the schools have added a massive corps of administrators, largely to deal with the demands of government agencies.

Academia, enabled by government largesse, also exhibits the phenomenon called "the edifice complex"—a compulsion to erect impressive buildings just as an institution is at the point of decline. Satirist C. Northcote Parkinson regarded a new and luxurious headquarters as an infallible sign that an institution is entering decline. By that test, the entire American university system is on the edge of decay.

One result of the favoritism for academia is that furious, broke, and miseducated students join the Occupy Wall Street movement to demand—wait for it—a yet larger Big SIS. It is like the old joke, "Why do you want change? Aren't things bad enough already?"

The tax system is a huge waste of brainpower. The National Taxpayers Union points out that the income-tax industry occupies "more workers than are employed at the five biggest employers among Fortune 500 companies—more than all the workers at Wal-Mart Stores, United Parcel Service, McDonald's, International Business Machines, and Citigroup combined." The net social value of all this work is—zero.

The tax system also creates huge uncertainty for taxpayers, especially businesses and investors. Between 2001 and

2010, the tax code absorbed approximately 4,428 changes, including an estimated 579 in 2010 alone ("code" means the basic statute, not counting changes in regulations or guidance documents). In early 2010, the tax code contained 3.8 million words, up from the 1.4 million words it had in 2001.

At a more general level, money that is channeled into subsidies for political favorites has not only a direct budget cost, but a huge opportunity cost. The budget does not reflect the cost of losing the businesses that never started because they could not get capital, or were aborted because of the uncertainties created by subsidy programs. The white-elephant convention centers that litter urban America, along with the let's-subsidize-millionaire-athletes-and-billionaire-owners sports stadiums, are monuments to special-interest-caused decay. They will be joined by acres of idle windmills and junkyards full of subsidized electric vehicles. Not so visible will be the ghosts of the viable businesses that could have been created with the same money, had they not been preempted by crony capitalism.

An iron law of Big SIS is that it must protect vested interests against the disruption of the future. Existing interests have money and votes. Those that may exist in the future do not. So Big SIS will always enlist on the side of stasis, sucking out of the air the oxygen needed for innovation. The reaction to the crises of the past few years is a telling example. Bankrupt business models such as the auto industry and green energy need restructuring, not an endless stream of government guarantees.

Big SIS also has troublesome impacts on the distribution of income in the United States.

A standard theme in current political controversy bemoans the inequality of income in the United States. Many of the claims are based on dubious premises. For example, households at the top of the income distribution curve have several earners and higher levels of education. Their members are married, often to other high earners. Households at the bottom often have *no* earners, less education, and unstable family life. Any rational economic system will reward those who are functional and productive, and give less attention to those who are not. The dysfunctional are appropriate objects of help and charity, but their incapacities cannot be allowed to dictate and distort the basic structure of society's institutions.

So beware of statists bearing tricky numbers. Their real purpose is to set up systems whereby they are paid to redistribute the income, and you can bet that the salaries they collect to perform this function will put them at the top of the distribution curve. Of course, this will then make the shares even more unequal, and this will become the basis for new claims about the imperative of redistribution, and so on.

The demand for fat salaries for those who redistribute income highlights a broader point about the effect of Big SIS on income distribution. Progressives like to blame inequality on "deregulation" and "tax rates". A competing explanation is that the expansion of Big SIS makes those skilled at manipulating it more valuable, and puts the squeeze on the rewards available to those who are not politically connected.

Has the pay of corporate CEOs boomed because it has become harder to run a large company or because the political connections necessary for successful crony capitalism have become more valuable than management skills? Many venture capitalists can make money by shrewdness, but there is only one Al Gore; by adding him to your team, you can collect half a billion dollars in government subsidies for an electric vehicle. Many people could run GE, but only Jeff Immelt was able to establish a personal relationship with a president and become chair of the President's Council on Jobs and Competitiveness. A general pattern emerging from the news reports about green energy is the political connectedness of the companies reaping the subsidies.

The financial industry is under attack from all parts of the political spectrum for its cozy relationship with Big SIS. A theme is *Wall Street Isn't Winning—It's Cheating*, because it profits from the financial guarantees and other favors. A financial columnist addressed a letter to a Wall Street tycoon explaining why people hate him:

> America hates unjustified privilege, it hates an unfair playing field and crony capitalism without the threat of bankruptcy, it hates privatized gains and socialized losses, it hates rule changes that benefit the few at the expense of the many and it hates people who have been bailed out and don't display even the slightest bit of remorse or humbleness in the presence of so much suffering in the aftermath.

Big SIS also effects the division of returns between capital and labor, to the disadvantage of the latter. Former Office of Management and Budget Chief Peter Orzag, now ensconced as a VP at Citibank, recently worried about the increase in the share of the national income going to capital. He blamed the Republicans, of course.

Consider an alternative: that the growing expense and risk that Big SIS imposes on employers who are hiring workers encourages the employers to substitute capital for labor whenever possible. The investment climate may not be good, but if an ongoing enterprise must be supported and the choice is between capital and labor inputs, capital looks like the safest choice. Big SIS might steal some of the capital, but at least the loss is limited. Adding labor creates open-ended obligations that are both incalculable and hard to shed.

Big SIS is particularly hostile to investments in resource extraction and industrial production, which range from coal to oil drilling in the Gulf of Mexico, to the Keystone Pipeline, to shale gas in Ohio. The energy extraction sector has, historically, been an important source of high-paying jobs for skilled, blue-collar workers. Discouraging investment pushes these people down the economic ladder.

Partisans of Big SIS invoke inequities of income distribution to argue for yet more government intervention. When the inequities are actually caused by Big SIS, intervention becomes a perpetual motion machine. Increasing crony capitalism, discouraging hiring, and hobbling investment exacerbates inequality, which is then used to justify more intervention.

Economists spend their time debating the Keynesian multiplier: what is the effect of government spending on overall economic activity? They should think more about the Big SIS divisor: how much does the government distort and reduce private activity?

In 2000, Jonathan Rauch compared graphs of the growth curve in the number of lawyers and advocacy groups with the decline in productivity-per-worker growth since 1973. His conclusion was, "The period of hyperpluralism and the period of slow growth roughly coincide." Since he wrote this, the rate of growth in influence peddling has expanded even faster, the nation's rate of real economic advance has declined further, and the misallocation of resources has proceeded apace. His hypothesis is looking good.

More broadly, Big SIS intrudes itself into civil society in a host of ways that cannot be captured by any economic analysis. America is a complicated web of social and economic institutions. These include private governments such as homeowners' associations and coop boards. Also included are various specialized organs of government, such as sewer or irrigation districts, that exercise dominion over a resource or activity. Then there are businesses, trade associations, professional associations, religious institutions charities, schools, and on and on.

These institutions are run according to complicated sets of principles that are different from those at work in ordinary government. Some, such as businesses, are based on market discipline. Some, such as trade associations, involve complicated "co-opetition", a mix of competition and cooperation. Some answer to standards and ethics of professions. Some are based on dedication to the values of scientific inquiry or to the imperatives of a religious faith. Special governmental districts are usually established to manage a common resource (e.g., irrigation), and they have their own special rules to protect all the stakeholders.

These institutions are not free of politics. My father, the son of a Methodist minister, began and ended his career in academia, with a sojourn in the middle in the Central Intelligence Agency. He said that for sheer spiteful intensity, church politics were the worst, followed by academia, with the internal infighting at the CIA a long way back in third place, and the politics of the political system in fourth.

But all these institutions are factions, not microcosms of the whole polity. So they can and must reflect a balance of interests and considerations different from those at play in national and state politics. Their values, standards, and objectives are their own, and their internal politics different from those of the overall political system.

When Big SIS gets involved, it recasts these once-independent institutions into Little SISes, which are then required to reflect the constellation of interests of Big SIS. This deprives them of the ability to carry out their own purposes, to their own loss, and society's.

Take a simple example: the 55-mph speed limit. Speed limits, when first adopted, were based on the calculations of traffic engineers concerned with safety, and conveyed information to drivers on the topic. By the time of the double nickel, which lasted from 1974 to 1995, the enterprise was dominated by True Greens and anti-energy fanatics, who wanted to control driver behavior regardless of safety realities. The result was that speed limits became useless as safety information and were treated with contempt by drivers, who knew that the 55 mph limit had nothing to do with driving and everything to do with special interest capture.

The same anti-energy and True Green forces have taken over and corrupted climate change science, as Big SIS pours money into subsidies directed at showing that there must be a serious problem. No skeptics need apply.

The health care system has been turned into a cockpit of battles over reimbursement levels, insurance requirements, and approved treatments and is conducted in the halls of Congress, state legislatures, the Department of Health and Human Services, and the Food and Drug Administration according to the rules of cost accounting rather than medicine.

Big SIS turned the mortgage business from a responsible mechanism for financing home ownership into a catastrophic experiment in social engineering. Then, to prove that contamination, once unleashed, is unbounded, it wrecked the financial system as well.

The student loan system started as a sensible way to allow those without money capital to invest in their own human capital. Big SIS corrupted it into a massive subsidy for its clients in academia. In pursuing this goal, the government encouraged academia to engage in unsustainable investments in both plant and staff. It also encouraged the institutions to dumb things down so as to meet the demands of students who were in school to get a degree rather than an education. Many students invested not in human capital but in consumption of froth, both intellectual and alcoholic, that did not equip them to earn money in a competitive economy. Now they must repay the money borrowed for this binge, but their earning capacity is paltry.

Energy production has been turned from a business based on hard-nosed calculations of the costs and benefits of the hefty long-term investments necessary into a gamble on political prediction and influence. Engineers can make reasonable assessments about the potential of oil, gas, wind, or coal fields, and an analyst with a spreadsheet program can assess the financial aspects. Rational investment decisions are possible.

Political winds are more difficult to predict. Making the payoffs from energy investment incalculable by rational analysis ensures that one of three results will occur: (1) Investments will not be made; (2) Investments will be made only by those who can corrupt the political system to ensure long-term profitability; (3) Investments will focus on creating shell companies that will collect subsidies, transfer the money to insiders, and then fold.

Given the rate at which green energy companies are going bankrupt, option number three is looking like the winner.

All these examples lead to one dreary conclusion: once Big SIS starts to corrupt any system of society, its own internal logic ensures that the corruption will grow.

These complaints should not be taken to mean that the corrupted institutions are innocent victims. Their operators are often eager participants, as the intervention of Big SIS can mean big money. Mortgage companies, university trustees, venture capitalists turned venture socialists, and trade association presidents swarm Capitol Hill, the White House, and K Street, begging to be tossed into the briar patch. Indeed, yet another corruptive effect of Big SIS is that other institutions start selecting their leaders for an ability to accommodate and milk Big SIS rather than for excellence in upholding the values of the institutions themselves.

Unfortunately, the proper functioning of these institutions for the benefit of society depends on their operators and members responding to sets of incentives that are different from the incentives governing Big SIS. The executives begging to be enfolded by Big SIS do not serve the long-term interests of their institutions and of the larger society.

Pondering these impacts of Big SIS on the non-government sectors of society leads to a conclusion pleasing only to those with a taste for bitter irony. The Progressive Movement hoped to reduce the influence of special interests on government. What it actually accomplished was the reverse. By setting in motion the limitless expansion of the power and responsibility of government, it contaminated every other institution with a Big SIS focus on special interest politics. Moreover, it corrupted the other institutions not with the venal corruption of petty bribery but with the systemic corruption in which benefits are fed back into the political system.

"This isn't fair dealing"

The Declaration of Independence was not a disquisition on monarchy or a discussion of theoretical objections to kingship. After a brief statement of principle affirming that governments are made to serve the ends of the people rather than vice versa, the Founders embarked on a list of grievances against George III, specific acts that caused them to say that this king had forfeited his legitimacy, his claim to obedience and loyalty.

This focus on practical performance is a sensible way to judge a government. Leave aside the political theories; do its actions make sense or does a reasonable person look at them and say "that's nuts" or "that's just *wrong*"? By its fruits ye shall know them, and if a political system consistently produces strange and disturbing results, it has a fundamental problem, whatever its underlying political theory may be.

Writing a bill of particulars about the current state of government would require a piece of paper considerably longer than the Declaration. Judging by the harvest of recent news clips, the number of incompetent, unjust, and downright weird decisions, both great and small, is overwhelming.

Furthermore, one cannot say, "Oh, that was just a mistake and they fixed it". Part of the pathology of Big SIS is that little ever gets fixed because almost every "mistake" was actually intended by some faction, and every reform can be blocked by some interest. Mistakes, once made, become irretrievable.

Here are some reports that trouble us Saxons standing in our furrows:

- The 1970 Defense Appropriations Bill had a dozen earmarks; the 1980 bill had 62; the 2005 bill had 2,671.

- As a part of the 2009 recovery program, the Labor Department spent $163 million to train workers on "Green Jobs". Of the 47,000 people enrolled in training, 26,000 completed it and 8,000 found jobs. Only 1,366 were still employed six months later. So the cost was over $121,000 per job.

- A court decided that the Chipotle restaurant chain violated the rights of the wheelchair-bound because its counters were forty-five inches high. This meant that a person in a wheelchair, unlike other patrons, could not see his burrito being made, which the restaurant advertised as a part of the Chipotle experience. So the court decided that the counters must be only thirty-six inches high. Question: would any rational person, given a pot of money with which to help the disabled, allocate it to cutting down the height of the counters in fast food restaurants?

- The Sarbanes Oxley Act imposed huge paperwork requirements, which seriously burden business, especially small business, for uncertain benefits. Nine years later, congressmen continue to posture about how awful this is; something must be done! Nothing happens, but it is good for campaign contributions.

- Let us lump together the stories of children operating unauthorized lemonade stands and the increasing number of SWAT raids on innocent citizens.

- Stephen Greenhut, the editor of *Cal Watchdog*, says "revolt is brewing" in rural California as livelihoods "are under attack from federal regulators and environmentalists" and, "when resource-related jobs leave rural areas, there aren't many other ways for residents to earn a decent living. Society collapses, and poverty expands. There aren't enough tourist-oriented gift shops to keep everyone gainfully employed."

- A long-term care program was included in the health care act, largely because its structure of collecting premiums immediately and paying out only after seven years made the law score better for the Congressional Budget Office. Everyone knows this was a charade, but the scoring system stood. In late 2011, HHS said it may drop the program. On the other hand, the administration declines to recommend its repeal.

- Blogger David McElroy witnessed a scene that might have come from the famous Ayn Rand novel *Atlas Shrugged,* as a businessman reacted to a public meeting on economic development in Alabama : "What I saw today is a broken process and a sham. We all want a decent environment in which to live...[but] the modern equivalent of a kangaroo court...isn't the way to go about it."

- A corporate executive commented on fundraising numbers for the 2012 election: "At this point, Wall Streeters really do not like Barack Obama. It has been a long time since I have met one who still actually supports him. But...the big financial firms know that their future profitability requires that President Obama influence [the Dodd-Frank] regulations, and he is exploiting that for all it is worth."

- EPA continues on its policy of shutting down fossil fuels, radically reducing electrical generating capacity, and making energy as expensive as possible. The future stability of the power grid is in question. The Administration also shuts down drilling in the Gulf of Mexico and watches the deep sea rigs depart for Brazil.

- The Administration declares war on coal, which is the cheapest energy source. The result will be that the coal companies ship the coal to China, which will then use it to cut the costs of the manufactured goods they ship to the United States to levels that render U.S. manufacturers uncompetitive, partly because the U.S. companies do not have access to this cheap energy source. The Administration also "delays" consideration of the Keystone Pipeline (after three years of studies), and "delays" gas shale extraction in Ohio for more studies.

- The government spends massive amounts of money to subsidize "alternative" sources of energy. At the same time, it does not promote nuclear power, which is the only logical way of protecting against climate change, should that risk be real, without impoverishing ourselves. (I am a strong skeptic about the magnitude of the climate change problem, but that is not relevant to the nuclear issue.)

- In terms of tax breaks, one of the most subsidized industries in the United States is the video game industry.

- Democratic moneyman and billionaire George Kaiser said, in 2009, "There has never been more money shoved out of the government's door in world history and probably never will be again than in the last few months and the next 18 months. And our selfish, parochial goal is to get as much of it for Tulsa and Oklahoma as we possibly can." He succeeds, becoming a major backer of Solyndra, the solar panel company that sinks in 2011 with a cargo of one billion dollars in federal loan guarantees. It remains unclear how much of the federal money was siphoned off by the insiders.

- The Fish and Wildlife Service, which administers the Endangered Species Act, believes that no cost is too great to ensure the survival of any species, however trivial—and however dubious the evidence that it is actually endangered. Some of its actions have been:

  ✓ During the 1980s, in the name of preserving the spotted owl, the government stopped harvesting timber on public lands and inhibited the use of private acreage, shut down hundreds of sawmills, and impoverished whole communities in the Northwest. Forward to 2011: The spotted owl is still steadily declining. The FSW does not know why but thinks maybe $127 million could bring it back. (It has no opinion on bringing back the defunct logging communities.)

✓ In California's Central Valley, huge tracts are deprived of water by the need to protect the Delta Smelt, a fish that is important only in the Gaia philosophy that no species should ever disappear. A federal judge recently excoriated the government for bad science.

✓ Also in California, in the early 1990s, FSW listed the California gnatcatcher as "threatened", which forced severe restrictions on land use across 197,000 acres in San Diego, Orange, Riverside, San Bernardino, Los Angeles, and Ventura Counties, with an FWS-estimated cost of over $900 million by 2025. A public-interest group requested delisting because the gnatcatcher is the same species that lives in profusion in Mexico. FWS made no reply.

✓ In 2011, FSW moved to protect the Dune Sagebrush Lizard, an action that might well shut down most economically productive activity in West Texas, including oil and gas production.

✓ FSW recently raided the Gibson Guitar factory, confiscating materials and records and causing serious harm, because it claimed Gibson was using rare Indian woods that, under the law of India, could be processed only by local workers.

India does not agree. The upshot: FSW is enforcing foreign labor laws that the foreign government does not believe were violated. After the affair received extensive blog coverage, FSW doubled down with new allegations that Gibson had imported unfinished ebony fingerboard blanks under the category of finished musical instrument parts. The public defense of his company by Gibson's CEO was cited to show that he was aware of the heinous nature of this offense.

- A homeowner replaced an old chain-link fence with a more pleasing aluminum one. The historic preservation commission protested. Although the old fence was quite ugly, it was historic because it reminded people how poor that part of the city once was. Atlantic's Megan McArdle commented: "I didn't think that the elements of privilege and classism already inherent in these historic preservation districts could be made more obnoxious, but boy, was I wrong."

- The government pays about $3 billion per year to 20,000 U.S. cotton farmers. In 2010, the World Trade Organization ruled that these violated free trade agreements. The United States responded by giving Brazilian farmers $147 million in subsidies.

- On farm policy generally, subsidies have cost $262 billion since 1995. Ten percent of the farmers collect 75 percent of the money, and 62 percent collect nothing.

- From 1999 to 2010, the number of liens filed by the IRS increased from 168,000 to 1,096,000, while revenue from the Collections Division remained flat. IRS often fails to properly code payments received from taxpayers under lien. It has also refused repeated requests by the National Taxpayer Advocate to moderate its lien-filing policies. It has no way of knowing if its practices, which are very damaging to citizens, have any effect on collections.

- In 2007, the Supreme Court ruled that carbon dioxide is a "pollutant" under the Clean Air Act and that EPA should regulate it. Recently, EPA requested relief from parts of this legal requirement, noting that its full implementation would require 230,000 new employees at a cost of $21 billion to issue 6.1 million permits. This problem, an unavoidable consequence of the Supreme Court's decision, was not mentioned in the Court's 2007 opinion.

- In 2005, the FTC forced Blockbuster to abandon its hope of acquiring Hollywood Video because of fear of monopoly in the video rental market. Blockbuster went bankrupt in 2010. Hollywood Video was bought by another company, which went bankrupt in 2010.

- The Equal Employment Opportunities Commission sued a trucking company for refusing to continue to employ an alcoholic as a truck driver.

- Toilets and showerheads continue to be subject to flow restrictions. A ban on incandescent light bulbs is decreed. Asthma inhalers are outlawed. None of these decisions can pass even a back-of-the envelope cost-benefit calculus.

- The Department of Justice brought criminal charges against oil companies because twenty-eight migratory birds landed on waste oil ponds, and died. The birds were not members of any endangered species. Windmills kill 440,000 birds per year, including many rare ones, but no action has been directed against these.

- Post 9/11, the Department of Homeland Security became a giant slushpot, giving $34 billion to localities all over the nation, regardless of risk. A cost-effectiveness analysis found that, to be considered cost-effective, DHS expenditures would have to foil up to 1,667 attacks each year of roughly the magnitude of the one intended on Times Square in 2010. The new HQ for DHS is being built on the site of the former St Elizabeth's hospital for the insane.

- Buried in the middle of the 2000+ pages of the Dodd-Frank Act is a provision requiring companies to disclose whether they use any "conflict minerals" from the Congo. Compliance will cost billions of dollars. Benefits are probably nonexistent. Nor does the provision have anything to do with the events that triggered the financial crisis.

- Also in Dodd-Frank, the Durbin Amendment required the Federal Reserve Board to cap fees that banks charge merchants for debit card usage. It was imposed via the influence that large retailers wield over one Senator and smuggled into the law during conference. Again, the law has nothing to do with the financial crisis, and the benefits are dubious and probably negative because the law interferes randomly with a complex financial ecosystem. After the Bank of America announced that it would now assess charges on customers for use of debit cards, Durbin denounced this, too, as though he were not responsible for the shift.

- In 1962, the junk science book *Silent Spring* triggered anti-DDT hysteria that led to a ban, until the Bush Administration ended it in 2006. The ban caused tens of millions of unnecessary deaths. In 2011, the Department of Justice sponsored a showing of the movie made from the book for its employees.

- In regulating wetlands, the Corps of Engineers follows a policy of refusing to provide clarity about its classifications and permitting policies. The policy lets the Corps assert jurisdiction in dubious cases and use the threat of horrific penalties to bludgeon owners into spending substantial sums on restoration or offsets regardless of the merits of the corps' position.

- The government often enters into civil settlements with firms accused of wrongdoing that require payment of substantial sums to private groups chosen by the government. Most recently, a Department of Justice settlement with Citibank appears tailored to channel funds to the infamous ACORN.

The inexorable logic of Big SIS

The snapshot of Big SIS presented in this chapter is partial and fragmentary. We really have no tools for assessing the extent to which it has taken over not only government and our economy, but also our civil society, or of estimating just how long a comprehensive parade of horribles would stretch.

Two points are significant, though.

First, precision is not really necessary. However uncertain our knowledge, it is good enough so that we should be appalled. We have reversed the idea that we are a people with a government and have turned the government into the dominant partner.

Second, this state of affairs follows relentlessly from the collapse of our political philosophy, as discussed at the end of chapter 2. The U.S. political system no longer has any set of principles that dictate that some actions should not be within the ambit of government. Lacking any mechanism for setting limits, the pressures of special interest activism will continue to expand it. Revisit any recent State-of-the-Union speech and you realize that the potential reach of Big SIS is limited only by failures of the human imagination to dream up new ways to control the behavior of others or to grab resources for one's own faction. Such failures are rare, because humans are very inventive when it comes to greed for either wealth or power.

This chain of logic leads to the conclusion that the continuing growth of Big SIS is inexorable. "Inexorable" is a word rich in connotations, mostly unpleasant. It means "relentless" or "unavoidable" or "cannot be moved by persuasion or entreaty". It is often coupled with "doom" or "fate".

So the next two chapters turn to this broader issue: is the logic of Big SIS truly inexorable, to the point of political doom, or can we escape it?

Chapter Four

Diagnosis and Prognosis: Big SIS Tomorrow

The zombies are at the gate

The Introduction likened Big SIS to an army of zombies attacking a civilized city. This chapter builds on that metaphor. It examines the gaps in the defenses of our democratic republic that the zombies are exploiting.

The focus is on prediction: is the rather bleak picture painted by the chapters assessing the history and current status of Big SIS truly justified? We are a resilient society. What will happen if we wait to take action? Will the natural defenses of our civilization check the trend toward an ever-bigger and more dysfunctional Big SIS and produce, if not perfection, at least a tolerable equilibrium?

The answer, unfortunately, is that business-as-usual is not a promising strategy. As foreshadowed at the end of chapter 3, the internal dynamics of Big SIS lead inexorably to expansion, not equilibrium. There is no reason to believe that these destabilizing pressures will ease.

Our political mechanisms are experiencing multiple failures, and serious reform will require sustained, deliberate effort. This chapter identifies ten gaps in our walls through which the zombies are coming.

The ratchet

Gap number one is that Big SIS is a ratchet. Anyone who has used this tool knows the routine. You pause to collect energy, exert yourself to move the mechanism forward a notch, and then rest to regain the energy to do it again, secure that you will not lose ground. An escape lever does allow you to ease the tension, but the normal state of the machine is to prevent any backsliding.

Big SIS tends to allow motion in one direction only—toward greater government activism—and then locks. Reversal is possible, but it is difficult and rare. In the Big SIS ratchet, once a special interest gains a subsidy, regulation, or advantage of any sort, it gains the benefits of the stasis built into our governing mechanisms by the Constitution.

The result is perverse. The comment to Congress by Justice Scalia quoted in chapter 2 lauded the effect of gridlock in preventing bad laws, but he ignored the crucial corollary. Once bad laws—or bad regulations, or successful captures of a budget appropriation or entire agency— *are* in place, the ratchet makes correction extremely difficult.

Part of Madison's theory about building a Constitution was that broad democracy would protect against capture by any faction. The multiplicity of interests would make it impossible for any one of them to gain sufficient political power.

This protection does not work when an interest can win by capturing just a portion of the government while most people are thinking about something else. Once that happens, the forces that initially inhibited action now favor the interest. Opponents are hard put to gather the support necessary to release the escape mechanism and reverse the ratchet, while the interest needs only to maintain a blocking position. Further, the interest is highly motivated and focused, while the public is usually watching the football game.

The special interests almost always win these contests. In *Government's End,* Jonathan Rauch described the repeated failures of reform efforts undertaken by both parties over periods of years. Attempts to end subsidies, to restructure, and to abolish agencies all failed, and the reformers wound up in disgrace. Big SIS is remorseless against those who threaten it.

A good recent example is the phase-out of incandescent light bulbs that began on January 1, 2012. It was the product of a coalition of bootleggers (manufacturers that will profit greatly from the new bulbs) and Baptists (True Greens). Few measures in recent history have been subject to as much scathing commentary or so completely exposed as asinine. But the supporting coalition is powerful, and the law has not been repealed. Indeed, the system is achieving the worst possible result. It produced a last-minute delay that may or may not become permanent, enacted a mere two weeks before the deadline, when the investments necessary for the transition have been made. The result is complete uncertainty.

Logically, the public should have the good sense to hold a grudge against the crony capitalists and their congressional pets and to punish them for this action. However, light bulbs are low on any citizen's list of priorities, and memories will be over-written by more important events. So the lesson for the interests is: win, and you can ride out the storm.

Defenders of small government count it a victory when they stop the ratchet from moving another notch. This produces delay, at best, but the zombies are patient. Sooner or later, an opportunity will present itself, often in the form of a crisis, and the ratchet will shift another notch—or, in a big crisis, many notches.

Indeed, in recent years, the barriers to reversing the ratchet have grown stronger, despite the obvious unhappiness of most people with the trend of events. In 2011, a supercommittee of Congress was created to try to find some cuts in the bloated budget. It failed, after superlobbying from affected interests. Of the lobbying legions, one hundred were former employees of supercommittee members.

The public's rational ignorance

Gap number two is called "rational ignorance".

Most of the time, most people do not keep track of the details of government. The level of attention declines steadily with the distance between an area of policy and a person's immediate daily concerns.

Pundits harrumph that the public fails to devote lavish amounts of time to studying up on public affairs (i.e., reading the pundits), but the effort would be a waste. Individual voters affect national affairs only occasionally—at voting time—and the force of a single vote is trivial. To spend large chunks of one's life to "become informed" would be of small benefit, especially given the low quality and high bias of most reportage and commentary. Thus, for any individual citizen, even one with a deep sense of civic responsibility, the rational approach is to remain slightly informed and rely on intermediaries.

It would be equally inefficient for rationally ignorant voters to judge candidates by their detailed positions on "the issues". Except for a few crucial topics, voters expect *the candidates* to spend their time studying the issues and to have deeper views on them than the voters have.

When you need your car fixed, you don't study auto mechanics. You go to a garage where they know more than you do. When you need your government run, you don't study up on every issue. That would waste time that can be more profitably and enjoyably spent on your private affairs. You hire a politician who *does* study the issues. In either case, the question is how to pick your expert. For a garage, talk to friends and check the websites. For politicians, it is almost the same but with less focus on technical competence and more on picking one who shares both the voter's overall values and sense of priorities.

This rational behavior by the citizenry has a downside when it is exercised in the context of a hyperactive state that wields a powerful regulatory apparatus. The system becomes vulnerable to vague, grandiose laws that appeal at a feel-good level while avoiding attention to the hard trade-offs that characterize the real world.

After the vague law passes, the decisions are shifted down to the bureaucrats in an agency. There, the impact of any specific decision, and thus the potential political backlash, can be limited. An individual legislator can also deny responsibility, campaigning on how he or she is heroically trying to rein in those damn, out-of-control bureaucrats, while privately assuring the interest-group supporters of the program that nothing will change as long as the interests keep contributing to the legislator's campaign.

Voters who are not immediately affected by the law will believe the public assurance, and even those who disbelieve will find it impossible to mobilize public support against what is now a *fait accompli.*

The Endangered Species Act (ESA) is a fine example of how the game of vague-smiley-face-law-combined-with-broad-delegation is played. As professor Jonathan Adler says, it was enacted in 1973 "with much fanfare and little controversy" because "few anticipated how broadly the law would affect both government and private activities."

In 1978, in *TVA v Hill* (the snail darter case), the Supreme Court said, "The plain intent of Congress in enacting this statute was to halt and reverse the trend toward species extinction, whatever the cost." It may have plain to the Court, but before the decision it had not been plain to anyone else. Nor did the public understand that the species to be saved "regardless of cost" included not just poster-child species such eagles and grizzlies but also every variety of rodent and fish.

The ESA has had limited success at preserving species. It has been quite successful at destroying Pacific Northwest logging communities and California's Central Valley agriculture, and it is now turning its guns on Texas.

Let us be clear about an important point. Under the Constitution, the federal government could declare species preservation a crucial public purpose and then use its power of eminent domain to buy up the California Central Valley or all of West Texas.

The government does not do this because the backers of the program know that requesting a budget item of billions or trillions of dollars to buy Central Valley or West Texas would fail in Congress. They also know that putting the "at any cost" proposition to a national referendum would lose.

Thus, their strategy was to pass a feel-good law, let the regulators impose costs on a few people at a time while keeping the level of those costs uncertain, and use the courts to expand the regulators' power. They would then rely on the forces of propaganda, inertia, and rational ignorance to keep the program going—despite the absurdity of the premise that Congress *really* intended that every species must be saved no matter what the cost to actual people.

The advocates and administrators then traduce those objecting to any specific application as attacking the feel-good purpose. To question whether the ESA should be used to protect the Delta Smelt regardless of its devastation to California agriculture is equated with a hatred of nature, or at least a hatred of eagles and grizzlies.

The proponents do not offer to share the economic burdens. During the spotted owl controversy of the 1990s, as whole logging communities were shut down to protect the habitat of the owls, Westerners bitterly suggested a law that would force DC residents, starting with congressmen, to open up their spare bedrooms to homeless people. No one took them up on it.

Then—there is a crucial final step. The regulators must have sufficient political sense not to press their power to a point that provokes a serious political backlash. The public's ignorance must remain rational. It is no accident that the East, especially near Washington, is largely free of large-scale damage from the ESA. Members of the congressional committees that supervise the Fish and Wildlife Service are also shielded from its costly attentions, as their states have fewer species listed as endangered.

The ESA is far from unique. The game of feel-good laws, murky costs, open delegation, and rational ignorance has been highly successful for over fifty years in many contexts. It is played repeatedly by the environmentalists. Chapter 3 mentioned the EPA legal brief noting that the True Green interpretation of the Clean Air Act requires an additional six million permits and 231,000 employees. The brief is unusual in that it recognizes the true implications of a law instead of relying on pap. But the problem was acknowledged only after it was too late to affect the interpretation of the law.

The environmental movement should not be singled out, though, because the strategy of feel-good laws backed up by broad delegation, politically savvy enforcement, propaganda, and staged outrage is, alas, typical.

The same dynamic is at work in the field of corporate governance and financial reform. Sarbanes Oxley imposed huge costs for uncertain benefits. Dodd-Frank was a response to a legitimate need for some new governmental powers to allow for orderly liquidation of failing financial institutions, but the result was a more-than-2300-page bill drafted largely by various special interests (including anti-capitalist "consumer groups") that requires five hundred regulations and dozens of studies and reports.

Included in Dodd-Frank were the conflict-mineral provisions mentioned in Chapter 3 and the Durbin Amendment, written by lobbyists for big retailers, which limited debit card fees and is forcing banks to revamp their checking services, often to the detriment of low-income customers. Other provisions were inserted, too, and there is a growing literature on the nasty surprises that were inserted in the bill during the panic about "financial reform".

The template of feel-good law plus delegation is used for the great entitlement programs, with their automatic funding increases and for which any effort to slow the rate of expansion is labeled "a cut". It is used for the Americans with Disabilities Act, which defines as "discrimination", and thus morally reprehensible, many problems that the differently-abled have functioning in a world that assumes full functional capacity. Because Americans are generally a fair people who are opposed to "discrimination", the political benefits of getting an outcome tagged with that label are immense.

The public is also generous, and, in the abstract, it is likely to agree with the judges in the *Chipotle* case, described in chapter 3, that it would be nice for a customer to have the full experience of seeing his burrito constructed. A rationally ignorant person, reading about the case with only about 10 percent attention, will not consider the downside of the increase in costs. If you phrased the question about the outcome another way—perhaps as, "Should minimum-wage workers in unrelated industries be forced spend more at *Chipotle* so that the wheelchair-bound can watch their burritos being made instead of served at their tables?"—the result would be different.

People would also be less sympathetic to the case's real-world outcome if you calculated the costs of complying with the burrito mandate, and then asked, "Given a budget of that amount, is the best way to help the disabled to spend it on raising the counters at Chipotle restaurants?"

In surveying the landscape of government, you find everywhere this pattern of broad, vague laws implemented by detailed regulations that impose murky costs on the private sector, with little attention to rational assessments of costs, benefits, or effectiveness.

The dynamic is self-reinforcing. As more rules are created, and as complexity and opacity grow, it becomes more difficult to be "well-informed". The rational response is not to increase one's efforts but to cut them back, becoming even less diligent in seeking knowledge. As the public grows more ignorant, the vulnerability of the system to propaganda and lies grow apace.

So the more that rational ignorance leads to bad government, the more rational it is for the public to become even more ignorant, and the worse the government gets.

Further, as Rauch wryly concluded, when political hackery confronts the spirit of reform, the public rallies—but usually to the wrong side. The protectors of special interest privilege find it easy to spook the people, who in the abstract want reform and leaner government but "not at the expense of students, farmers, bankers, workers, veterans, retirees, homeowners, artists, teachers, train riders, or cats or dogs."

The interests' knowledge and rapacity

Gap number three is that the special interests are rationally knowledgeable.

In contrast to the rationally ignorant public, it is well worth the interests' while to understand the details of legislation and programs, and the more complex these become the better for the interests. Complexity adds to the advantage of those who do understand the programs, because the more difficult it becomes for the public to form a judgment the easier it becomes for the factions to win with propaganda.

Complexity is also valuable to the legislators, who can remain ignorant of the workings of the laws and programs they create, secure in the certainty that the public cannot know enough to call them to account.

The edge in information and understanding held by the special interests has dire consequences because these organizations have no incentive to limit their demands. As Mancur Olson noted, an interest gets the benefits while the costs are borne by society at large, so there is "no constraint on the social cost such an organization will find it expedient to impose on society in the course of obtaining a larger share of the social output for itself." Interests will impose very large costs to obtain trifling benefits.

The incentives for unbridled rapacity work even more relentlessly on the agents and representatives of interests than on the members themselves. A principal might have some sense of restraint, however slight. The representatives earn their money by being unreasonable, and justify themselves by a professional ethic that binds them to demand things for their clients that no decent person would demand for herself. The representatives have neither a mechanism nor an incentive to limit their demands to accommodate either the reasonable needs of other interests or the good of the public, except when compelled by political forces.

In any case, making strong demands is usually good business for the representatives. Retainers do not roll in unless the principals are aroused by either greed for gains or fear of losses, and the agents must generate a story about why one or the other is imminent. The Washington term for it is "juicing the troops", and neither nuance nor honesty is a job requirement.

Special-interest greed takes many forms. While everyone is familiar with the concept of capture of agencies by those with an economic interest, ideology equals money as a motivator. Government programs can be captured not by economic interests but by true believers in particular causes who get themselves named to run the implementing agency. Indeed, total belief in an agency's mission is usually regarded as a job requirement by Congress. It is rare for anyone who expresses any reservations whatsoever to become head of an agency, especially because the relevant committees in Congress are always dominated by true believers, or by members who want to profit from the campaign contributions of the true believers. Given this going-in position, the willingness of government administrators to consider seriously any values other than their organization's principal mission is usually between small and zero.

Control of an agency can also be used as a bastion from which to raid surrounding territory, because its authority can be stretched to apply to situations remote from its immediate responsibilities. Again, the environmental field provides a golcanda of examples. Many defenders of endangered species care more about stopping development than about the actual species, and see the Endangered Species Act as a means to this broader end. They will stretch the law's meaning to and beyond its limit, regardless of the benefit to the supposed purpose of species protection. Repeated studies about the mediocre success of ESA in saving species are irrelevant to them because the law is working beautifully, from their perspective, by freezing land use.

Wetlands regulation follows the same model. To the program's champions, discouraging development and extorting resources from landowners to devote to environmental protection are as important as protecting wetlands. They deliberately create uncertainty about the definition of wetlands and make a determination of a parcel's status into a difficult business. To be a wetland, land need not actually be wet. It is enough if the land is wet sometimes, or maybe if it is has plants that sometimes grow on land that is wet, or if it is near wetlands. Penalties for violations are horrendous. So landowners agree to pay for remedial measures or offsets rather than litigate for years, and they count themselves lucky to be allowed to use their land at all.

EPA recently announced a program to promote "environmental justice". Companies already in full compliance with all of EPA's requirements will nonetheless be pressured to do more for the community in some unspecified fashion in the name of promoting undefined principles of justice for the benefit of unnamed local groups. The implicit threat is that companies failing to cooperate will find their permit applications assigned to the slow track and their inspections even more nitpicking than usual.

Chapter 3 told of the indictment of the oil companies for the demise of twenty-eight migratory birds in North Dakota, an action that appears to be in this category of expanding authority in the interests of a broader agenda. The purpose is not to protect birds but to hobble fossil fuel production. The action is especially droll considering that windmills are now killing half a million birds a year, mostly in the same part of the nation. Because wind power is regarded as environmentally correct, this avian massacre does not count.

In talking about extensions of authority, we should not neglect the grandest of all—the use of government-sponsored enterprises to guarantee mortgages for low-income buyers, which converted the GSEs from financial institutions into income redistributors, with disastrous results.

The inventive special-interest representative can find further ways to leverage an agency's power, because a narrow faction can exploit the clout of a more powerful group. For example, the Department of Education is the preserve of the very powerful education industry. But there is another, narrower special interest in Washington: the branch of feminism that seems to assume that all intimate interactions between men and women are the equivalent of rape. In a campaign that has received little mainstream attention, this interest is trying to leverage the power of the agency to force universities to rewrite the rules of evidence used in cases of alleged sexual assault, moving to a "preponderance of the evidence" standard that, in practical effect, automatically declares the defendant guilty if he is charged.

This is a fine example of the type of exploitation by faction that Big SIS enables. The necessary power already exists in general laws. The precise issue is complicated and requires considerable background to understand. Opponents of the change are easily smeared as "pro-rape" or "anti-woman", and those who will suffer in the future are unknown and have no incentive to protect an interest that they do not know they have. The threat to the colleges is loss of federal money if the demand is not complied with, a very serious concern.

The lesson is that if you, as an advocate for a narrow interest, can capture the right slot in a powerful agency that has bigger clients with serious clout, then you can do wonders for your cause. In other words, capture can be leveraged by means of a subfaction capturing a faction which captures an agency.

As special interests become more successful, society as a whole, especially the economy, is coming to resemble an overgrazed national pasture. The more the livestock of one interest chomps the grass, the less is left for the others.

Logically, you might think this would create incentives for everyone to pull back and rethink, but that is not how the incentives work. The collisions among the special interests over which ones get to graze on the pasture and the rising realization that the whole system is becoming unstable creates incentives for every interest to become even *less* restrained.

Game theorists call the phenomenon "the last period problem". An impending end to a state of affairs or a contest increases the incentives for greedy behavior because there is no incentive for long-term husbandry. If the commons is becoming overgrazed, each industry finds it rational to eat all the grass before the others get it rather than pull back so the pasture can renew itself.

You often see last-period behavior in a business that is nearing insolvency. As the situation worsens, each stakeholder tries to grab more for itself, and the cooperation necessary to refloat the enterprise becomes harder to achieve.

The same dynamic exists in government. So, as our current crises intensify, the propaganda becomes more shrill. The level of client-directed activity at regulatory agencies increases, and so does the resistance of special-interests to cuts in their shares of the budget pie or to limits on their regulatory authority.

A commercial by the AARP crossed my TV screen recently. It showed an army of grim seniors telling politicians that they "have earned" their social security and Medicare, and they will remember at election time anyone who trifles with it.

The term "earned benefits" is fairly accurate for social security in recent times. (Early recipients were paid far more than they put in.) For Medicare, it is not. For past retirees, Medicare has been a bonanza, with 1980 retirees getting up to $18 per dollar contributed, and current retirees in line to get from $2 to $6 per dollar of contribution.

The accounting can get complicated, however, because the straight contribution-versus-benefit ratio does not take account of time and the rate of return on money or inflation. Receiving $2 now for $1 put in thirty years ago is not a good deal.

The point, though, is that AARP makes its money by convincing seniors that it is their militant champion, and it has little incentive to educate them on the complexities of who is getting what from Big SIS. Indeed, the more intransigent the representatives, the better. Not only does this appeal to the membership, but it warns the politicians to pursue some softer target if they want to cut the budget and not to look to the seniors to be part of the solution.

The game theorists have an adage for this ploy, too: "Well, *you* must give in, because *somebody* must be reasonable if we are to avoid disaster, and it is certainly not going to be me."

AARP knows the game well, but so do all the other special interests in DC, so nobody plans to be reasonable. Thus, intransigence is not just rational; it is essential. Any interest that confessed, "Well, we could take a bit of a haircut" would soon find itself shorn bald while all the other interests retained their long, curly locks. Politicians, like all predators, smell weakness.

Noise in the system

Gap number four in the defenses of the democratic republic is that "Laws, the most wholesome and necessary for the public good", as the Declaration of Independence put it, get lost in the noise of special-interest advocacy.

The Declaration, after an opening two paragraphs of political philosophy, moves into a bill of particulars against King George. The first three items on the list refer to his obstruction of necessary laws, not to bad acts he has performed, with the language quoted above at the top of the list.

The general welfare of the nation requires laws and regulations. Conservatives are often accused of hating government or wanting weak government. Not so. Conservatives want government to be strong, but they also want it to pursue a limited number of projects that promote the general welfare, not to be a source of payoffs to special interests. They want government to focus on things it can do effectively, not on incompetent efforts to act as a national nanny. They oppose "game-show government", which means: "Vote for us, and we'll give away cash and prizes. We'll send you a check!"

As chapter 2 documented, a difficulty in holding to the values of the Old Republic during the nineteenth century was that industrialization, population growth, and urbanization created a continuing need for new legal arrangements. Because of the novelty of the circumstances, the political and judicial systems found it hard to distinguish factional from general welfare legislation.

Nonetheless, the period was creative. Before the 1830s, corporate charters were special privileges granted by the legislature. The nineteenth century developed general incorporation, which made the corporate form available to all. The society then invented the bodies of corporate law that were essential to creating the large pools of capital needed by the increasing scale of industry and markets.

Reorganization in bankruptcy was devised to meet the needs of the beleaguered railroads. New systems of workers' compensation were a rational reaction to the poor fit between the rising heavy industries and conventional tort law. A new body of automobile codes emerged. The West needed specialized water law that reflected the needs of an arid region rather than the doctrines of the soggier East, land law that reflected the invention of barbed wire, and mining law. Both consumers and honest producers demanded protection of food and drug laws against adulterants that could be downright fatal.

The Progressive historians and their progeny have planted in the public mind the idea that if the producer interests of society seek a law, it must be antithetical to "the public interest". Certainly, producers sometimes seek advantage, but laws are necessary for the smooth functioning of the economy, and an automatic distinction between producers' interest and the public interest is specious.

When I worked for the Federal Trade Commission, the Bureau of Economics would sometimes argue that an action proposed by the attorneys should be rejected because it would reduce economic efficiency. The lawyers would yowl, "But that is the industry's argument!", as if anything supported by producers must be bad. It is a strange mindset, but it permeates the government bureaucracy, not just the FTC.

A democratic republic must meet the challenge of making the crucial distinctions between factional advantage or corruption and the general welfare, and laws that help the producers be productive should be at the top of the legislative to-do list.

Big SIS obliterates our collective ability to tell the difference between good and bad. The seeking of advantage is so ubiquitous, and the general level of discussion is so low, that good proposals and bad look about the same. Businesses themselves have lost the ability to distinguish between laws that would help the general welfare, incidentally advantaging the business itself, and laws that sabotage the general welfare for the benefit of the business. Everything is argued in the same superficial and misleading terms.

The Sunlight Foundation, which promotes government openness and is on the whole a very useful organization, put the "return on lobbying" to large corporations for one action at "22,000 percent". Reading the fine print reveals that the action sought was to let companies bring foreign-earned profits back to the United States without paying punitive taxes. The action sought was actually profoundly in the general welfare, and the real scandal was that the companies were forced to spend lavishly to overturn bad tax law.

At the free-market think tanks in Washington, a frequent complaint is that Big SIS has destroyed the ability of producers to advocate good policies and that business cannot be counted as a champion of free markets. Firms argue their own short-term advantage and shun any serious analysis of effects on the free market because they fear that it might damage their advocacy next year, when their management might want some free-market-destroying special favor.

The producers themselves lack a compass to tell them when they are on the side of the angels and when they are not. In my time as a think-tank analyst, many a post-mortem on a meeting with business interests reached a bemused conclusion: "They don't seem to understand that they have a good argument because their position would in fact promote the general welfare. They think they are corrupt even when they are not."

Unfortunately, the legislators have adopted the same "there is no truth" approach to the world and see every vote as for or against some collection of interests rather than in terms of good or bad policy. In this, they are encouraged by the press, which views all proposals through the same lens of special-interest capture and is concerned primarily with which interest benefits from a particular decision.

For the press, this mind-set extends to the Supreme Court. Most reports of decisions focus on which interests won and lost, not on an analysis of the issues involved. Because the press is mostly leftist, the headlines often take the form of "Supreme Court hates women" or some similar travesty of reason. This debases the political dialogue still further.

The ratio of the noise of Big SIS to the signal of concern for general welfare has become overwhelming.

Compassion traps

The news media went agog over a hypothetical question posed during a 2011 debate among Republican presidential candidates. The issue involved a healthy young man who declined to get health insurance and then showed up at a hospital with a life-threatening condition. Should he be treated?

The candidates avoided a "let him die" response, saying that of course our compassion would not allow this, so he should be treated, and so on.

This generosity exemplifies a phenomenon called "a compassion trap", and gap number five for the zombies is the large and rising number of these.

Because we as members of society are too sensitive to let the young man bear the consequences of his deliberate choice to remain uninsured, we must pay to treat him. The effect is that he has manipulated us into insuring him for free.

Once you start thinking along these lines, you see that the political system is full of compassion traps, situations in which our collective sensitivity as decent humans and our reluctance to see people endure pain even if it is caused by their deliberate decisions sets up our own exploitation, locks us into destructive societal systems, or both.

The hypothetical example of the young man's refusal to buy health insurance is an obvious case. Something similar arose in real life when a homeowner who had refused to pay an annual $75 fire department fee was then outraged when the firemen refused to put out a fire in his house. The owner said that he offered to pay the fee on the spot, which indicates he had a dim grasp of the concept that one should purchase insurance in advance, but some progressive bloggers were appalled by the tough-minded stance of the fire department, even though, logically, it would seem optimum to let homeowners decide for themselves whether they need the protection or not and then abide by their decision.

Compassion traps come in many guises. Crop subsidies are one. The value of the subsidy becomes part of the price of farmland. The person who profits is the landowner at the time the subsidy is implemented. The current farmer receives only a standard return on his capital and labor, but ending the subsidy would do him great harm by reducing his income and whacking the value of his land; thus, once a subsidy system starts, we are stuck with it forever.

The war on drugs is a compassion trap. Because we are too sensitive to let people harm themselves, we create large paramilitary forces, send thousands of young males to jail (disproportionately minority males who, with different incentives, might provide much-needed entrepreneurial energy to our cities), and remit billions of dollars to some of the nastiest people in the world, who use it for other evil purposes, such as terrorism. We also clog the courts and prisons and expand the intrusiveness of the criminal law apparatus, as battling drugs requires nasty tactics that are then transplanted to other areas of law enforcement, like a particularly unpleasant invasive species.

The war on drugs shows how bad things can get when a compassion trap is reinforced by a powerful bootleggers-and-Baptists coalition. The drug lords and the anti-drug police have strong common interests in the system.

Welfare of any kind becomes a double compassion trap, snaring both the donors and the recipients. The right to any benefit must be phased out at some income level, because otherwise everyone in the nation would be entitled to it. Whatever the income level chosen for the cap, from the standpoint of the recipients the loss of the benefit works like a tax. If several benefits are lost at a particular level of income, then the effective tax rate on additional work can exceed 100 percent. So people get trapped below that level even if, with the right encouragement, they could rise far above it. And the rest of us support them in this failure because it would be cruel to cut them off.

Because of this dynamic of discouraging self-help and improvement, compassion traps create a learned helplessness in the recipients that destroys them economically, physically, and spiritually. Another example in the news now: Extending unemployment benefits with no retraining requirement turns the currently unemployed into the long-term unemployable.

Compassion traps put us on the horns of a dilemma. It is difficult to distinguish between the genuinely unlucky and their honest and compassionate representatives, and the sociopathic and their often equally sociopathic representatives. Without intrusive controls and requirements, which do indeed burden those in need, we leave ourselves open to endless manipulation by people who are skilled at exploiting compassion and guilt.

Then, because we are compassionate, there is good reason to approve everything and end nothing. Compassion traps are tolerable when there are only a few of them but overwhelming when they multiply—and they do keep multiplying. Any welfare program triggers demands for its expansion. To someone aggrieved at seeing others obtain benefits not available to him, the logical response is not to organize to oppose the program. This would be difficult, and the savings would benefit all taxpayers, not just his own group. The better course is to organize to expand the program to include oneself and one's fellows. This triggers further envy from others, of course, and inspires them to organize to expand the benefits still further.

Our reaction to compassion traps leads us to expand Big SIS in other ways, as well. A logical response to the young man who refuses to insure is to control his behavior by forcing him to buy insurance. This prevents both his efforts to free ride on the rest of us and the affront to our sensitivity of watching him suffer.

Once he enters the system, though, Big SIS will quickly see and seize the opportunity to exploit him as a cash cow. Healthy young people need few medical services, and by lumping him in with less healthy populations we can jack up his premiums to subsidize others.

To be more specific, we can reduce the premiums paid by the elderly, who vote in large numbers, and make the youngsters chip in to cover their Viagra, hair transplants, hip replacements, and other desires. After all, we are much too compassionate to force elderly men (who are on limited budgets and are now, due to other government policies, earning no interest on their hard-earned lifetime savings) to pay for their own penis pumps (a $250 million item for Medicare over the past decade), or for the hair transplants required if they are to have a hope of needing the pumps.

The health care example is, of course, the current ObamaCare litigation. The government claims a right to force individuals to buy health insurance precisely because we are collectively too compassionate to let them suffer. The government will not put *quite* so much stress on the desire to use them as cash cows, but the briefs in the case make clear that the requirement that the healthy purchase insurance at a premium rate is essential to the law's coverage of the sick at a reduced rate.

Is this a great country, or what? The more sensitive we are the more we get to control people's behavior and redistribute their resources, and the more we can make health care and other systems respond to the politics of special interests rather than customer demand or market reality.

A final problem with compassion traps is that they are quirky, because our collective compassion radar is bizarrely selective. We have the attention span of a goldfish, which according to urban legend is so short that every trip around the bowl is a new experience. The public may weep over one healthy young man who might have to bear the consequences of his free choice, but it yawned while millions of African children died of malaria because Rachel Carson's junk science book *Silent Spring* stampeded us into a ban on DDT.

Even when we recognize them, though, compassion traps are hard to resist because at the point of decision there are no good choices, especially when the "for the children" card is played. Special interests and the advocates of a big welfare state know that they are hard to resist, which is why they work so hard to create as many traps as possible. They have extensive experience in this and are very skilled, so compassion traps multiply and resist not just reform but even rational discussion.

At the same time, even as we grudgingly give in, those of us outside the ambit of beneficiaries and system operators know that we are being cozened and resent the governing class's failure to develop rational responses.

Moral claims

Gap number six consists of moral claims.

Viewed in terms of political calculation, reliance on a moral claim has an overwhelming advantage. If the claim is acknowledged by society at large, then its presenters short-circuit public resistance to factional legislation. That a program focuses on helping a particular group is the purpose, not a defect. The American public's sense of justice, combined with guilt over its denial, is a fount of great political power.

The Progressive Movement and the New Deal both appealed to morality, bringing to politics a fervor that was almost religious. The activists were not just adjusting an economy, but righting wrongs, even if to the skeptical eye of a time-distanced observer their claims often look like special interest pleading.

To this day, labor tries to ride the narrative of power imbalances that started during the nineteenth century, a tale of the excesses of capitalism and the need for government intervention on the side of the workers to level the playing field.

The Civil Rights Movement had a powerful narrative of compelling morality, one that has been replicated by many other disadvantaged and victim groups.

The environmental movement had strong appeal to rationalists who were offended by the free-riding inherent in pollution. It also appealed to a spiritually-oriented clientele, who turned environmentalism into a form of religion, a substitute for the declining conventional churches. Groups within the movement differed in their focus, but they agreed that environmentalism had a moral basis beyond any utilitarian calculus.

The moral claims of the labor, civil rights, and environmental protection movements resonated with the public, suffused them with great political legitimacy, and became critical components of Big SIS.

The supporters and professional advocates for these interests know they have a successful strategy working and continue to rely on the interests' status as moral claims to deflect accusations that they are just another special interest and to demand ever "more" from society.

Moral claims are hard to resist, but they pose a danger because, as longshoreman-philosopher Eric Hoffer may have said: "Every great cause begins as a movement, becomes a business, and eventually degenerates into a racket."

All three of these interests have fallen on hard times in that their moral claims are being challenged.

Labor's claim to need favors as an offset to the power of capitalistic behemoths disappeared with the decline of the large smokestack industries that gave rise to Big Labor in the first place. Steel, autos, printing, airlines, and other giants have deteriorated markedly, often largely because of inefficient work rules and excessive pay imposed by unions.

Arguing that a power imbalance exists is difficult when the unions have enough clout to destroy their employers. It is even more difficult when the union movement consists largely of public employees. As of 2010, unions had 7.1 million private sector members and 7.6 million from the public sector. Because the private sector is much larger, the percentage of all workers in the sector belonging to a union was 6.9 percent for the private sector and 36.2 percent for the public.

Government employers are by definition not the evil capitalists of legend, and the news accounts hammering public sector unionism for excessive pensions, mediocre local services, and failing schools also undercut the narrative of moral superiority.

The Civil Rights Movement has also lost considerable moral authority. In a society that elected an African American president, and in which organizational elites work overtime to identify and promote competent minority candidates, it is hard to argue that racial prejudice cripples the opportunities for minorities. One could make a good case for affirmative action in the 1960s, but the rationale has thinned in the decades since, and now it is doing its supposed beneficiaries more harm than good.

The public is coming around to the view that too much of a once-proud movement has degenerated into another special interest. And that too many of its leaders are eager to maintain their followers in a compassion trap rather than bring them into full participation in society.

Environmentalism is also in a strange place, morally.

From the start, the movement overstated the benefits of federal regulation; pollution in the United States and everywhere else has declined steadily for decades as wealth has increased. The rate of improvement did not shift much after the deluge of environmental laws, though a curve of the costs would certainly show a steep rise.

Because of the movement's strong religious component, the True Greens have been pushed into difficult positions, advocating irrational and destructive policies to respond to tiny or illusory risks. Even proposals that might make sense as long-term strategies become destructive when pursued as crash programs. In any case, the movement has plucked the low-hanging fruit and is now past the point where returns are negative. For example, pending proposed reductions in mercury will require annual compliance costs of $11 billion while producing $6.1 million in benefits, by the agency's own estimates.

Increasingly, the environmental movement is seen more as having an agenda that is anti-development, anti-energy, anti-modern, and, indeed, anti-human rather than pro-environment.

Naturally, all doubts about the moral supremacy of the claims of these groups are furiously rejected by their advocates. Much of their power within their own organizations depends on maintaining their clients' sense of outrage, and they do not want to lose their leverage on the political system. So they continue to play the card of moral outrage whenever they are challenged. And it continues to work well enough to roil our politics.

The Regulatory State rampant

Gap number seven in our defenses is the loss of loss of legal and administrative control over the Regulatory State.

The Regulatory State is based on the delegation of broad but ill-defined power down to administrative agencies. It is an essential component of Big SIS.

In theory, three of our great institutions should check regulatory excesses: the Courts, the Presidency, and the Congress. All have failed. If you want a single villain, though, blame the legal profession as an institution, because it has performed poorly for several generations. Baffled by Big SIS, it has removed the safeguards against faction put in place by the Founders, and without them, in the words of law professor Glenn Reynolds, "It is no surprise that the tendencies they guarded against have grown, any more than it is a surprise when someone whose immune system has been suppressed develops infections."

With a few exceptions in the courts of appeal and in academia, the legal profession's doctrines of administrative and constitutional law are stuck somewhere back in the 1930s. The current generation of lawyers was mis-educated about the history of the values of the Old Republic described in chapter 2, and bought into the Interest Group Liberalism theories of the New Deal, along with the "government must have power to solve national problems" theme. They failed to understand the nature and danger of Big SIS, and the incomprehension has crippled their response because it relies on "defer to experts" or "defer to democracy" bromides that refuse to examine how the sausage really gets made.

The Supreme Court has occasionally said "there comes a point where this Court should not be ignorant as judges of what we know as men" (or women, to update). Nonetheless, the Court seems to be determined to ignore most political developments since the New Deal. The models of administrative law used by the courts are based on New Deal platitudes about disinterested administrative expertise, which were based upon Progressive Era platitudes.

The Supreme Court never uses the school of analysis called Public Choice, which starts with the premise that politicians and administrators are not dedicated purely to the public interest but, like actors in the private sector, seek their own advantage. It never uses the concepts of collective action or of game theory, and it never heard of the work of Mancur Olson.

As recounted in chapter 2, the courts mostly abdicated their role in controlling legislatures in the late 1930s. They will uphold any legislative action dealing with economic affairs as long as it has a "rational basis", but rational basis means only that the legislature says that a problem exists and that the law is directed at it. Neither the underlying facts nor the logical links will be examined, and any legislature that flunks this test is composed of total idiots.

Other constitutional clauses could have provided some protection against predation by special-interest capture, but they, too, have been diluted almost out of existence. The Fifth Amendment prohibition on taking property without compensation retains some effect against overbearing regulation, but it is minimal; the loss of value caused by the regulation must be total, and governments are permitted to exhaust their victims through endless bureaucratic delays.

The courts' abdication of substantive review of regulatory affairs did not mean that they, presidents, or congress completely gave up on supervising the regulatory agencies.

Efforts started during the New Deal, culminating in the requirements of the Administrative Procedure Act (APA) of 1946. These seemed to work tolerably well until the great spate of legislation and regulation that started in the 1960s.

An asterisk should be put by the phrase "seemed to work". The workability was due largely to the agencies' ability to establish mutually beneficial relationships with client groups while keeping the toll on society below the attention of a rationally ignorant public. The APA was at root a charter for regulation under the theory of Interest Group Liberalism, and its focus was to create orderly processes through which the interests could interact.

Establishing orderly processes was useful and important, but it was not adequate to the challenges created by the expansion of social and environmental programs in the 1960s and 1970s. These upset the balance by making government far more expansive, expensive, intrusive, incoherent, and inconsistent.

Since this expansion, repeated efforts have been made to bring the Regulatory State under some degree of legal or administrative control. Success has been modest.

The biggest successes were in the 1970s, when powerful business interests, exasperated with the costs and inefficiencies imposed on them by existing regulatory systems, supported deregulation of transportation and telecommunications. A second success came in the 1980s, when economists from the pro-market Chicago school demolished the intellectual underpinnings of the antitrust regulatory regime and convinced the courts that the Chicago-school views were right.

Some further checks have resulted from the APA's mandate that courts should examine whether an agency action is within the scope of the legal authority given it by Congress and should bounce regulations that exceed it.

Another lever of judicial control came from the provision in the APA that agency action must not be "arbitrary" or "capricious". During the 1970–80s, the courts interpreted these words as requiring procedures designed to promote reasoned decision making and to give interested parties significant opportunities to participate. Agencies were told to explain their decisions, to put technical information on the record, to respond to cogent comment, and, in general, to interact with the public more honestly.

These limitations did and still do some good in that they keep agencies from going off completely half-cocked. They also somewhat limit the efforts by agencies to stretch their authority so as to achieve goals that lie outside their areas of responsibility and authority. A significant number of major agency rules get bounced back for more work,

But an agency can usually win if it persists, and they have learned to play the system. EPA hires contractors who recruit battalions of twenty-two-year-olds to read comments and compose "responses". I once made a telling point against a rule—irrefutable in its logic, in my never-humble opinion—and later looked at the contractors' report to learn why it was ignored. The total explanation was, "The agency does not agree."

The courts have also failed because the judges fear capture of agencies by producer interests. The concern is legitimate, but the vision is too narrow. Corporate America is only one source of special-interest capture and corruption. Public employees, True Greens, unions, agency staffs, political entrepreneurs, and other ideologues and interests are equally dangerous, but largely outside the ken of the courts.

Then, to double down on the judges' blinkered vision, concern about corporate capture never translated into effective mechanisms for dealing with true crony capitalism. Such expensive regulatory actions as the light-bulb ban, the low-flow toilet, and much of the structure of financial regulation remain untouched.

When agencies tried to escape capture by non-industry clients or public-interest groups, courts often restored the manacles. In *Chevron* (1984), the EPA developed market-friendly, incentive-based approaches to clean air regulation. The True Greens protested, insisting on a regime of rigid command-and-control rules, and won in the DC Court of Appeals.

The Supreme Court took the case and tried to rein in the courts of appeal by ruling that agencies have authority to interpret their basic statutes. A court cannot reverse the agency's view unless it is outside any reasonable reading of the law.

In the factual and policy context of *Chevron* itself, the decision was a check on Big SIS. But no good deed goes unpunished. No presidential administration since the 1980s has been interested in promoting market-based approaches at the EPA or at any other agency. So the agenc(ies) lost the immediate skirmish, but the ultimate result was that they ended up with more authority than ever, because they get to define the limits of their own power, with the courts acting as a check only if a definition is beyond the bounds of reason.

Chevron is an important case, the single most-cited Supreme Court decision in the history of American law. Not only did it shift power between agencies and courts, but it also shifted the allocation of power between Congress and the agencies.

Before *Chevron*, a significant function of the courts of appeals was to police the bargains reached by contending interests during the legislative process. Limits on the range of permissible interpretations of the law were tucked into committee reports and floor debates, and the compromises were enforced by the judges.

It was an imperfect process, because legislative history is often confused and conflicting, and judges could pick and choose which parts to rely on. Harold Leventhal, a well-respected DC Court of Appeals judge of the 1970s, called analyzing legislative history "the equivalent of entering a crowded cocktail party and looking over the heads of the guests for one's friends." Nonetheless, the judicial function of enforcing the bargains made during the legislative process was important, and *Chevron* diluted it, with complicated consequences.

Agency power was increased. So was the value to interests of capturing an agency's personnel, because the original understandings backstopping a law could be reversed in the future by the agency. Striking interest-group bargains during the legislative process became harder; a faction can protect itself only by inserting its protections into the words of the statute itself, so statutes became longer, more complex, and less flexible.

These trends make the system more opaque and expensive to understand, which in turns feeds back into the problems of rational ignorance and of political discourse as superficial propaganda. You can argue about *Chevron*, and there are weighty considerations on each side, but it is clear that the Supreme Court had limited understanding of the intricacies of the system it was disrupting.

If the regulatory branch of Big SIS has become less controllable by courts, it is still, in theory, subject to Congress. Congress sometimes tries, using stern lectures and occasional appropriations riders forbidding some inquiry that offends a special interest that has the ear of a committee chairman. Another popular tool is to require impact statements of many kinds, such as environmental impact statements, small business impact statements, and paperwork estimates.

Indeed, every interest now demands that Congress require an "impact statement" on the theory that this will force the agency to pay attention. Mostly, impact statements are another move in the old congressional game of loudly assuring the aggrieved that problems are the regulators' fault while whispering to the interests behind the regulators that nothing is going to happen. If action becomes imperative, a compensating payoff for the most powerful of the aggrieved can be arranged as an alternative to reforming the program.

Congress sometimes threatens to review regulations itself. The Congressional Review Act of 1996 created a mechanism whereby Congress could review major rules and, it was assumed, reject the unworthy ones. It has been used exactly once, in 2001, on an unpopular OSHA rule, and seems to be a dead letter.

The most recent proposal for congressional responsibility for the regulatory system is a serious effort. Called the Regulations from the Executive in Need of Scrutiny (REINS) Act and introduced late in 2011, it would require every major rule to be approved by Congress and the president. Its current prospects are zero, except as an issue in the 2012 campaign, but if it ever passes, it will be important because it shifts burden of momentum. An interest that procures a regulation at the agency level will no longer be able to rely on its ability to block and delay action, as it will need affirmative endorsement by Congress.

The president, in his institutional avatar of the Executive Office of the President, is a third source of control over regulatory agencies. In theory, a president represents all the people and thus has a perspective that eludes the more specialized visions of his subordinates, who focus on the particular interests of their clients.

Many of President Reagan's appointees in the regulatory agencies pushed for a more free-market approach, one less devoted to the interests of labor and True Green client groups. Some did well, but many were not well-prepared for their jobs, and victories were minor and transient. They were trashed by the mainstream press wing of Big SIS, harassed by Congress, distrusted by the courts, and largely neutralized.

For over thirty years, though, the Office of Management and Budget has persisted. OMB is continually upset about the inefficiencies and costs of regulation, and a series of executive orders have commanded improvements in cost-benefit analysis, established review offices, mandated publication of calendars and agendas, and made volumes of information public.

Again, these efforts at control have kept the situation from becoming even worse than it is. However, no president has established good control over the tide of agency rulemaking, except perhaps Bill Clinton.

Clinton's purpose was not to rein in the agencies but to unleash them. He co-opted the regulatory system and turned it into a major support of the coalition of special interests that kept him in office. He also understood the importance of not overgrazing the pasture. His goal, in addition to obtaining credit with various groups for helping them, was to dole out benefits without overstressing the system. His strategy was shrewd. He could talk center, regulate left, and count on the sympathetic lethargy of the press to evade notice. Clinton hid in plain sight.

Among George Bush's sins, in the eyes of economic conservatives and believers in property rights, was his habit of talking conservative in his speeches while ignoring the regulatory system. His beleaguered OMB officials exercised some check on captured agencies, but the inertia of the system is not easily resisted. Besides, Bush kept using the regulatory system to try to woo the left, to convince them that he was not really one of those crazy righties. Opportunities to ease burdens without sacrificing real environmental protection were missed in areas such as wetlands and endangered species, and good initiatives were suppressed for the sake of the cosmetics of the political needs of the White House.

The Obama Administration is like a less-sophisticated Clinton operation. It wants to use the regulatory system for special-interest ends, but it does not understand the problem of overgrazing the commons or the need for the White House staff to control the agencies. The overwhelming impression is one of special-interest-dominated agencies freelancing on behalf their clients, with no concern about sustaining the national pasture.

A fundamental reason for the failure of efforts to control regulatory agencies is that our legal institutions treat all agencies as though they were the same. Agencies are regarded as experts, told by Congress to tend to some particular garden that Congress lacks the time to deal with. This assumption misses a crucial fact, which is that the nature of the missions given to agencies and the incentive structures within agencies vary greatly, and the differences are important.

Some agencies are responsible for the health of an important economic sector. The Federal Communications

Commission has often performed badly and venally, but it has an incentive to ensure that the nation has a functioning telecommunications system. The Department of Energy may be a cockpit of special-interest infighting, but at the end of the day, its administrators fear that they will be held to account if the energy system collapses. The fear tethers the DOE to reality, however loosely.

Other agencies, including the Environmental Protection Agency and the Fish and Wildlife Service, lack any such responsibility for an economic sector. More broadly, they have no incentive to care about the national economy as a whole. On the contrary, the strongest clients of the True Green agencies would regard shutting down most industry as a worthy sacrifice to Gaia. Thus, the costs these agencies are willing to inflict on the world are limited only by outside political pressures, not by any internal gyroscope.

Every time you log onto a news website, you see evidence of this incentive structure at work. EPA is bootstrapping the idea that carbon dioxide is a pollutant to control fuel emission standards for automobiles, even though specific legislation is directed at this issue and would, a sane person might think, trump EPA authority. Unlike the principles governing the process under which the Department of Transportation considers fuel economy standards, EPA has no obligation to consider safety or economy.

The great labor agencies—the Department of Labor and its subunit, the Occupational Safety and Health Administration, and the National Labor Relations Board—are similarly blinkered in their views. They care primarily about union labor. They have been and remain willing to see employers exit business, at a cost in jobs, if that increases the returns to unionized workers.

The Department of Labor has an even narrower client base than union members themselves. Its clients are the executives who run unions. The agency regularly undermines disclosure requirements that might give the members information on how much their leaders take from them.

Health and Human Services has a dynamic of its own. Because of Medicare and Medicaid, every branch of the health care system is controlled by HHS reimbursement rates. HHS is not just a player in the system but the cockpit in which the multitude of affected interests struggle and negotiate.

You can go on down the roster of agencies, calculating their roles, powers, clients, and incentive structures, and finding complex and important differences. But nowhere in U.S. legal doctrine will you find a serious recognition of the importance of these distinctions or an effort to make doctrine reflect the realities of the differing incentives at work in the agencies.

Add up all of these problems and failures, and it is clear that, insofar as the future of Big SIS is concerned, the failure to devise effective controls on the Regulatory State is a gaping hole in the defenses of the republic.

The Ruling Class as a special interest

Gap number eight in our defenses is the performance of the Ruling Class.

In 2010, Angelo Codevilla, professor emeritus of international relations, wrote a widely circulated essay on *America's Ruling Class—And the Perils of Revolution.* Codevilla argued that the United States has developed a ruling class, a "court party" that cuts across the Democrat/Republican divide. Some of its members are in the government and some not, but the court party "speaks the language and has the tastes, habits, and tools of bureaucrats", and "rules uneasily" over the rest of us.

Around the same time, Arthur Brooks of the American Enterprise Institute wrote in *The Battle* that a statist, redistributionist coalition composed of 30 percent of the population is controlling the rest of us. And Richard Fernandez of *PJ Media* made a similar point in *Storming the Castle*, using the term "the Party of Incumbency". He quoted a plea by then-Majority Leader Nancy Pelosi urging Republicans to make common cause with the Democrats against the rocking-the-boat Tea Parties as evidence that the Ruling Class has common interests that transcend party identification.

In Codevilla's terms, the rest of the nation is the "country party", a heterogeneous collection of those who do not define themselves by their relation to government and who are "yearning to rule themselves rather than be ruled by others".

Codevilla's distinction is a good one. So is Brooks' point that the country party maintains the core value of the Old Republic that the government need not and should not be in charge of everything, or even of very much. It thinks the mainsprings should be the free market and civil society.

The court party embraces a different ethic, one skeptical of individual merit and free will. It tends toward a fuzzy conclusion that all wealth derives from the amorphous collective efforts of society, that there is no particular merit in producing wealth and that the immediate producers have no moral claim to it. Therefore, its allocation should be determined by society, which, of course, must act through its representatives in the government, who turn out to be (surprise!) members of the Ruling Class.

This ideology so suits the needs of the Ruling Class that one would call it heaven-sent, except that the class is too irreligious to believe in heavenly gifts.

The ideology puts the Ruling Class in a crucial role. I recall a novel in which three soldiers kidnap a tank. The hero announces that he must be the commander who looks out the top and gives orders. His logic is that the three jobs needed are driving, shooting, and commanding. The hero can neither drive nor shoot, and each of the other men can do one of those jobs. Ergo, the hero must command.

Many second- and third-generation members of the class make a similar claim: they must command because they are not trained to do anything else. They have expensive university degrees, but in soft subjects or in law. Their capacity for productive work in the private economy is dubious, and their interest nonexistent. Therefore, they must either join the government and run things or work for the special interests that orbit around the government.

Because the Ruling Class is entwined with the government, its wages are set not by a free market but by bargains with other members of the class. Government employees get better pay than private sector workers, and the ancillary contractors, regulatory lawyers, public interest groups, and academicians do even better.

Nor is the value of the output of the Ruling Class assessed by the market. Governments always elude market discipline, and the foundations, universities, contractors, and other ancillary institutions that have attached themselves to the government have attained the same happy state.

One definition of bliss is to have the value of one's work defined by the cost of the inputs rather than by the market value of the outputs. The cost of producing a law review article is around $100,000, which wildly exceeds any valuation that would be put on it by a market. Indeed, the value of many of these works is negative. They are not worth the value of the time it takes to read them, so on the whole their production reduces societal wealth. Good luck in finding this reflected in the national income accounts.

A multiplier effect is also at work. Much of the activity of the Ruling Class consists of reviewing and revising each other's work. Thus, the time spent by readers of an article, however useless it may be, enters the national income accounts as an output. Comments on the article can be prepared, and comments on the comments, and a never-ending chain of pseudo-value created.

Indeed, the Ruling Class seems to engage in an odd reversal. Only intellectual products, such as articles and papers, videos and e-mails, games and Facebook pages, are worthy of respect. Concrete activities, such as energy production, natural resources extraction, or manufacturing, are not important on their scale of values. One reason for the success of the True Greens in their long war on these activities is that they do not constitute the immediate economic base of the Ruling Class, which has been indifferent to their decline. Of course, Ruling Class members are dependent on the physical economy in the long run, but that is too remote to affect short-term decisions.

The Ruling Class is also skilled at creating allies. The Heritage Foundation has an Index of Dependence on Government, which uses 1980 as its base year. The index rises from 19 (1962) to 100 (1980) to 272 (2009). The higher the number of people dependent on government payments, the greater the level of support for government, especially as the proportion of people paying taxes declines.

The large cadre of people paid to influence or oppose government would, in the pinch, be horrified if government were actually to shrink. Lobbyists, especially former congressional staffers or executive branch employees thought to have clout with ex-bosses and colleagues, command high fees. When AT&T wanted to buy T-Mobile in 2011, it spent millions of dollars on lobbyists. Few of these were charged with writing learned white papers on the virtues of the merger; mostly, they crafted PR campaigns and visited congressional, Department of Justice, and Federal Communications Commission staff.

That the Democratic Party is the primary home of the Ruling Class is no surprise, but many Republicans are also comfortable with Big SIS. They just have different ideas as to which interests should be favored and who should control the ratchet. Tea Party supporters criticize many establishment Republicans on the grounds that they do not want to end Big SIS but run it.

When the chips go down on the table, it is a rare member of the Republican establishment that cannot be bought with a subsidy, as when the Chamber of Commerce endorsed the programs of cash for clunkers and tax credits for home buyers, both of which were thoroughly stupid ideas. A jape in Washington is that the Democrats are the evil party and the Republicans are the stupid party, but sometimes bipartisanship prevails and they do something both evil and stupid. (Sometimes the joke is told reversing the roles; it works either way.)

The Ruling Class itself is a great bulwark of Big SIS. Whatever the particular roles occupied by its members at any moment, Big SIS is the iron rice bowl, and protecting it turns the Ruling Class into a special interest all its own. Government activism of any kind, without regard to the underlying issue, creates jobs and status. The substance does not matter as long as there is continuing demand for administrators and the influence peddlers that orbit around them.

Serious reform would greatly upset the Ruling Class because it would throw thousands, perhaps millions, of people out of high-paying and high-status jobs. As the saying goes, "It is difficult to get a man to understand something when his job depends on not understanding it"; thus, it will be exceedingly difficult to get members of the Ruling Class to agree to dilution, let alone termination, of Big SIS.

Barriers to change are reinforced by the status of the mainstream press as a part of the Ruling Class. As Evan Thomas of *Newsweek* said before the election of Obama, the press is worth 10 to 15 percent of the vote to the party of statism in any election, and this is a large rock to roll uphill.

All things considered, the Ruling Class will resist any attack on its status right up to the point of serious crisis. Richard Fernandez of *PJ Media* attributes to members of the Tea Party the sentiment that "The sheer size of government was now working against it. The bureaucracies had drained the surrounds of sustenance and now, they were on the point of either finding new prey or cannibalizing each other to survive."

These commenters make a good point, though I question their timing. The zombies will eat everyone else before they turn on each other, so cannibalism will be the last resort.

Campaign finance

Number nine on the list of gaps in the defense of democratic republicanism is the perverse efforts at so-called campaign finance reform.

The conventional complaint is that there is too much money in politics and that we need to limit contributions, and so on. But as Bradley Smith, a former member of the Federal Elections Commission, wrote, "Almost everything the American people know, or think they know, about campaign finance reform is wrong."

Money and corruption are problems, but they are the consequences, not the cause, of Big SIS. As long as government agencies meddle in everything, passing out goodies and redistributing at whim, everyone must gather around to influence the process. Even those who would prefer to remain apart must join the game or be ruined, and extortion is more prevalent than bribery. The Washington saying is, "Be at the table or be on the menu."

Efforts to regulate campaign finance, sponsored primarily by leftist academics and advocacy groups, are not really directed at reducing the power of special interests. They are intended to gag criticisms of Big SIS so that special interests can be spared the inconvenience of principled opposition.

The high levels of delusion and mendacity that surround discussions of campaign finance regulation are enabled by an extraordinary level of complexity.

For example, you might think that every sensible business corporation creates a Political Action Committee (PAC) to influence public officials. Not so. Running a PAC is onerous, and only 2000 of the millions of companies in the United States have them. Logically, the companies that make the necessary effort are those most interested in government favors or most fearful of government wrath. The complex campaign finance regulations thus create a barrier that excludes from the political arena any companies that want to support broad pro-market policies that serve the public interest rather than their own narrow profit.

So, welcome to the bizarre world of campaign finance reform, where one important goal is to exclude anyone who *lacks* corrupt motives.

You might also believe, as a result of tides of propaganda, that the Supreme Court's 2010 decision in *Citizens United,* which upheld the free speech rights of corporations, was a decision for "business". In fact, Citizens United itself is a nonprofit organization that, according to its mission statement, "seeks to reassert the traditional American values of limited government, freedom of enterprise, strong families, and national sovereignty and security". It depends on contributions from like-minded citizens. It is a corporation only because almost all organizations in America are so-called corporations. The four justices who would have denied corporations the rights of free speech in *Citizens*

United actually voted for more corruption, not less, via the permanent ensconcement of Big SIS.

A few more facts enhance understanding of the relationship of the campaign finance reform movement to Big SIS.

One is that the rules are written by incumbent legislators. This is a classic fox-guarding-the-henhouse scenario. If only the pesky Supreme Court could be cowed into acquiescence, the incumbents would have a free hand to write the rules under which people try to unseat them. Any legislators who could not then protect themselves forever are too dumb to deserve to stay in office.

Another fact is that congressmen constantly complain about how much money campaigns cost and how much time they must spend raising it. But the cost is due to Congress' unbridled power. If people's lives and fortunes depend on appeasing the legislators, they certainly want to influence the decisions. The only cure is to reduce the value of the prize. It is not surprising that naïve businesses assume that the solution is to "take the money out of politics", but this cannot work, because as long as the threats are there channels of influence must and will be found.

The time devoted to fundraising is largely a product of contribution limits. The $1,000 limit on a contribution to an individual campaign enacted in 1974 remained unchanged until 1992, even as inflation eroded two-thirds of its value. The limit is now $2,500, equal to $540 in 1974 dollars, but it is now subject to an inflation adjustment.

Congress could raise these limits at any time. It chooses not to because, although the limits make an incumbent's life unpleasant, they make a challenger's life almost impossible. In 1998, political action committees gave $220 million to congressional races, of which 78 percent went to incumbents, 10 percent to challengers, and 12 percent to candidates in open-seat races. Similar ratios have prevailed forever.

Further, the companies with a big stake in crony capitalism, the only ones that find it worthwhile to form PACs, tilt overwhelmingly toward the incumbents who distribute the loot.

The next point is that business contributions can be regarded as a product of extortion rather than bribery, and companies often support limits on campaign contributions and expenditures because they hope to avoid the shakedown. The whole system is a combination of bribery, extortion, crony capitalism, and protection racket. Money might buy political influence, but political influence can also be used to obtain money and to force private parties to send streams of largesse flowing toward a politician's supporters and friends.

The limits on contributions make officeholders seek aid from every possible interest. A *quid* is necessary for the *quo*, of course, and, in addition to a promise of "access", the best *quid* for a legislator is to promise to block something the contributor wants blocked rather than to pass something. Blocking is easier and less visible. Besides, a proposal might not have passed anyway, so everyone can take credit, even if they had little to do with the outcome. As a bonus, an undesirable proposal can also be brought back next year, so it serves as a cash cow. Everyone in Washington is familiar with the concept of cash register legislation—bills introduced without serious intent, designed to force interests to pay up.

The game theory guys have another relevant concept here, called the "dollar bill auction". A dollar bill is auctioned off to the highest bidder, with the added condition that the second-highest bidder must also contribute to the pot in the amount of his last bid. The bidding quickly reaches a dollar—and does not stop. The person who bid $0.99 and then got outbid realizes that he should bid $1.01 for the dollar and lose only a cent, as stopping would mean a loss of $0.99. Then, the one who bid a dollar makes a similar calculation and now bids $1.02, to which the other must respond. And so on.

No logical end exists. In a real-world situation, the parties would eventually get together and agree to stop, splitting the losses. But in Washington, the parties are represented by influence peddlers who are taking money off the top of every bid, and they have no incentive to end the auction at any level or to explain to their clients the nature of a dollar-bill auction.

Indeed, the lobbyists and the legislators are in a tacit cabal to ensure that lots of legislation is proposed because this increases the opportunities for dollar-bill auctions. From the perspective of these players, the relationship of the proposals to the general welfare is of no interest. The important point is that some laws pass and some businesses get punished for failing to spend enough. In this twisted system, a few really bad outcomes are useful to ensure that business stays panicky. The more arbitrary, irrational, and damaging the system becomes, the better for the influence-peddling business.

The next point is that campaign finance laws are designed to hobble the basic Republican constituencies of small businesses and professionals by imposing contribution limits and limiting PAC creation, while allowing Democratic constituencies—including public employees, unions, entertainers, and Native Americans—to leverage their advantages.

Union members are a tremendous resource, especially public employees who can take a sick day on the first Tuesday of each November to turn out the vote. Unions also devote huge chunks of the dues they collect, often via automatic checkoff, to political causes.

Entertainers are exempt from normal contribution limits because they can provide "services". A star can perform at a benefit to raise thousands of dollars for a party or candidate. As a volunteer service rather than a monetary contribution, this is essentially uncapped. An entertainer can contribute his or her time for a fundraiser and draw in 10,000 people at $100 per pop. This nets $1 million for the campaign, at little cost to the entertainer. An industrialist, on the other hand, can contribute only a few thousands to a candidate, even taking advantage of every loophole, and must use his own money. Politicians spend a lot of time in Hollywood these days.

Indian tribes are exempt from normal limits on campaign contributions and are a leading funder. In the 2007–08 election cycle, a group of four California Indian tribes gave $130 million, more than any other donor. As a benchmark, the National Education Association, normally regarded as a big spender, chipped in only $56 million.

Rich Democrats, such as financiers, are allowed to support candidates without stint, via soft money and independent PACs, but so are rich Republicans. This one is not quite a wash, because more of the super-rich are on the Dem side, but it is close. Dynastic candidates of both parties are favored because they can rely on family address books and past favors while their opponents are prevented from raising the money to challenge them. Of course, the rich can spend unstintingly on their own campaigns, so a rich dynast is in true clover.

Viewed in this full context, the leftist assault on the *Citizens United* decision makes sense. The Democrats can dispense with citizens' organizations because they have other ways of organizing. The Republicans, and conservatives generally, do not.

In terms of the prognosis for Big SIS, the campaign finance issue is depressing because the public discussion is so distorted. A variety of polls show that the booming anti-*Citizens United* propaganda is having serious impact, as almost 75 percent of the public disapproves of the decision. Because the case was a 5-4 opinion, we are one Supreme Court appointment away from catastrophic changes in our campaign laws. And, as if to prove Jonathan Rauch's point that the public usually rallies to the wrong side in a propaganda war, three-quarters of the public would approve of the destruction.

Political legitimacy revisited

For gap number 10 in the defenses of democratic republicanism, return to political legitimacy.

To recap from earlier chapters, the sense of legitimacy—the right to rule, the "claim...to the obedience and loyalty of their citizens/subjects", in Professor Beer's words—is the glue that holds polities together against the centripetal forces of fragmentation and disorder. Once legitimacy starts slipping, it feeds back into further loss of legitimacy in a descending spiral. Without legitimacy, there is no basis of government except habit, which lasts only as long as times are good, and if loss of legitimacy goes far enough, when a crisis comes then the polity shatters, and the source of power become sheer force.

In the play *A Man for All Seasons*, Thomas More's son-in-law says he would chop down England's forest of laws to get at the devil. More rejoins, "[W]hen the last law was down, and the Devil turned 'round on you, where would you hide...do you really think you could stand upright in the winds that would blow then?"

Substitute "political legitimacy" for "law" in the quotation, and we are back with Professor Beer's class, time traveling to societies in crisis. Once political legitimacy is chopped down, the winds do indeed blow hard.

The bedrock of political legitimacy in our system is consent, as expressed in the Declaration of Independence: governments are created to secure the "unalienable Rights" of "Life, Liberty, and the pursuit of Happiness", and these governments "derive[e] their just powers from the consent of the governed".

Only 20 percent of the respondents to a recent Rasmussen poll said that the federal government today has the consent of the governed.

Gallup polls show the same level of disillusion. A poll in September 2011 found that "a record-high 81 percent of Americans are dissatisfied with the way the country is being governed, adding to negativity that has been building over the past 10 years."

Other highlights of the poll:

- 82 percent of Americans disapprove of the way Congress is handling its job.

- 69 percent say they have little or no confidence in the legislative branch of government, an all-time high and up from 63 percent in 2010.

- 57 percent have little or no confidence in the federal government to solve domestic problems.

- 53 percent have little or no confidence in the men and women who seek or hold elected office.

- Americans believe, on average, that the federal government wastes 51 cents of every tax dollar, similar to a year ago, but up significantly from 46 cents a decade ago and from an average 43 cents three decades ago.

- 49 percent of Americans believe the federal government has become so large and powerful that it poses an immediate threat to the rights and freedoms of ordinary citizens. In 2003, less than a third (30 percent) believed this.

Since 1973, Gallup has done an annual poll of public confidence in institutions. In 2011, the military was at the top of the list, with 78 percent expressing "a Great deal/Quite a lot" of confidence, 16 percent having "Some", and only 3 percent with "Very little". Small business was next, with numbers of 64 percent (a lot), 26 percent (some), and 8 percent (very little). At the bottom was Congress, with 12 percent (a lot), 40 percent (some), and 48 percent (very little). Scattered in between were other institutions, including churches, the medical system, big business, the presidency, the banks, and organized labor.

Americans are a skeptical lot, and it is hard to get to 50 percent on the high-confidence scale. Only the military, small business, churches, and police exceed this as a historic average, with Congress averaging 26 percent. Nonetheless, it is troublesome to see Congress, the presidency, and the Supreme Court all running so far below their past levels. Only the banks have sunk farther, with a current high-approval rating of 23 percent as opposed to an average of 42 percent.

Contradictory explanations of these results exist. Some might disapprove of Congress because it is dominated by venal, narcissistic timeservers who have lost sight of the values of the Old Republic. Others might be unhappy because Congress is failing to give enough money to their preferred special interests, such as themselves. Either way, these are bad numbers.

According to the Heritage Foundation's 2010 Index of Dependence on Government, 44 percent of people pay no income tax, though of course they pay payroll and other taxes. 21 percent of the population collects welfare payments of some kind, including Social Security and Medicare, and another 8 percent are directly employed by federal and state governments—at total of 88 million people that Heritage classifies as government dependent. The figures cited in chapter 3 about the number of people who rely on the government for their paycheck even though they do not work directly for it would raise the total of the government-dependent population still higher.

One cannot assume, however, that government-dependent people automatically support Big SIS. A high proportion of them are seniors. Of the 88 million identified as dependent by Heritage, half are in the "old age" insurance category (including me). These people do not to regard themselves as "on welfare", having been told for seventy-five years that social security is an insurance scheme. This mind-set is important, because their status as recipients of government checks does not automatically translate into generalized support for Big SIS and its works. In fact, it would be reasonable to bet that seniors are over-represented at Tea Party rallies.

Nonetheless, a serious risk is the creation of a governing coalition that supports the government precisely because its members believe the government has been captured by special interests and that they are net beneficiaries. Recent political reports suggested that this represents the strategy of the Democratic Party for the 2012 election—a coalition of the dependents and elements of the Ruling Class that ignores the interests of the producing class.

Left uncertain is where this coalition thinks the funding will come from. Being largely ignorant of numbers, they may assume that a stash of money exists somewhere or that the productive classes will always consent to be looted. In either event, support given to a government only by those it pays off is not a solid grounding for true legitimacy.

The participants in Washington power games do not think in terms of political legitimacy. To shift the metaphor of the commons from pastures to water, the interests do not see that legitimacy is a special kind of commons, a reservoir of general political authority that no sensible government or society fritters away.

In political affairs, some level of corruption and favoritism will be tolerated. The public cares little if the mayor's nephew gets the paving contract, if the project is actually necessary, the work competent, and the price only mildly inflated. But the tolerance has limits, especially as the number of unnecessary projects grows, along with the incompetence level, and the prices skyrocket. The limits are reached more quickly when the projects take the form of serious impositions on the public, ranging from revenue-producing red-light cameras to heavy financial imposts that are siphoned off to favored groups. In particular, no government can, consistent with maintaining its legitimacy, make unlimited demands on its people when it is obviously acting as a channel for factions.

Special interests do not care about protecting the reservoir of legitimacy. Few of their representatives even understand the concept. Try telling lobbyists for the light bulb makers that the ban on incandescent bulbs pollutes the national reservoir of political legitimacy. They will think you have gone mad. So will bankers, if you suggest that the resumption of generous bonus policies after the 2008 bailout sabotages the government's authority to deal with crises. So will True Greens, if you tell them that devastating California for the sake of the Delta Smelt undermines the republic.

Those who do grasp the point will probably respond: "Aha! A last period problem! We better grab all we can before others appropriate the government's remaining legitimacy for their own ends." Then they will rush to their offices to snatch even more for their clients before the system breaks down.

Demonization is too easy, though. The reality is that even if a particular faction wanted to act responsibly and to cooperate with others to achieve long-term solutions to current problems, it would be unwise for it to go first when it does not know whether other interests will reciprocate. If the politicians refuse to demonstrate leadership in recognizing the problems and developing the necessary bargains and trades, it is extraordinarily difficult for private interests to act. The situation is worsened by a mainstream press that attacks any politician who does act responsibly.

The question of legitimacy should be examined from another angle.

In this essay, the term has been used in the sense of the legitimacy of an institutional structure and constitutional regime. The term has another meaning. In common usage, it is applied to persons, as in "legitimate king" or "legitimate heir". This raises the question of the legitimacy of the Ruling Class.

We in the United States sometimes talk about the Mysterious East and the Mandate of Heaven—legitimacy is conferred by success, and its withdrawal is signaled by the triumph of a new warlord or the appearance of some calamity that engulfs society. We contrast this with our system, in which legitimacy is conferred by consent and elections, or, as argued in the discussion of history, by general acceptance of expertise or moral claims.

We should not kid ourselves. Americans believe in the Mandate of Heaven as much as anyone else in the world. We do not tolerate unremitting failure, and if the individual leaders thrown up by the system are incompetent, the people will decide that those leaders lack legitimacy and must go. We may not use the same words, but deep in our gut we believe that failure means that the Mandate of Heaven has been withdrawn. And if the leaders will not depart under the existing constitutional regime, then the system will be changed.

The past few years have not been kind to the claim of the Ruling Class that it possesses the Mandate of Heaven, as one policy after another has been exposed as nonsense and rapacity—housing; financial regulation; sellouts to government employee unions; expansions of tort liability; energy regulation; and the government takeover of the medical system. Pretty much wherever government has asserted the old Progressive/New Deal/Great Society need for total control of some segment of the society or economy, the ground has been sown with salt.

Blogger Monty Pelerin (a pseudonym) analogized government policies to "Kevorkian economics", as one societal organ after another goes on life support. His list:

- The banking system is insolvent and near collapse.

- Government debt is approaching its maximum, at least as far as arms-length buyers are concerned.

- The social welfare system is unsustainable, with record numbers of people on food stamps and extended unemployment benefits.

- Government revenues shrink due to actual and potential diktats from Washington. The uncertainty these create is not conducive to private initiative.

- The Social Security Fund is now cash-flow negative. Unless provisions are changed, it is unsustainable in the longer term.

- Medicare is broke and bankrupting the country. ObamaCare will dramatically worsen this black hole. Massive changes in these programs are necessary.

- Fannie Mae and Freddie Mac are insolvent and require continuing bailouts from taxpayers. The FHA is not far behind.

- The student loan program will be the next big bailout. Students are graduating with unprecedented levels of debt and unable to find employment.

- Government-run organizations such as Amtrak and the postal service lose money consistently. They cannot be effectively managed in a political environment.

- "Green energy" jobs are a myth and a new potential bubble. Subsidizing these jobs or "investments" is merely another political boondoggle and misallocation of resources. Ethanol subsidies are a prime example of this green uneconomic engineering.

The likelihood that our rulers, of either party, can reclaim legitimacy through successful micromanagement of the economy is zero. Everything they attempt is too riddled with special-interest favoritism to constitute a rational approach to anything. Look at the Dodd-Frank financial reform bill, which is 2000+ pages of special interest protection interlarded with vague delegations. Look at ObamaCare, most of which was written by various health care special interests.

Even if one believed in the Progressive Era doctrine of rule by disinterested, nonpolitical experts, these recent laws bear no relationship to that model.

So we have a Ruling Class that cannot possibly meet the expectations that it creates, that has a tenuous connection to the productive capacities of the society, but that clings avidly to its privileges because it has no line of retreat except downward mobility. It is difficult to think of a better prescription for loss of legitimacy.

Down the slippery slope

In a recent article, political scientist Francis Fukuyama rejected the suggestion that expansion of government should be feared as a slide down the slippery slope to "authoritarian statism". The past fifty years, he said, demonstrate that "the slippery slope has all sorts of ledges and handholds by which we can brake our descent into serfdom".

I must need new glasses, because these ledges and handholds are not visible to me. We could survive all sorts of expansions of government, even quite silly ones, if they were undertaken for the right reasons, such as support of free markets, production of real public goods, performance of vital core functions of government, genuine charity, or the better functioning of civil society, and if they could be corrected in case of error.

But the system cannot survive unstructured and unlimited activism whereby the government whimsically imposes rules because someone thinks they are a good idea or some ideological or corporate interest captures an agency, a program, or a piece of Congress, and all decisions, once made, are cast in concrete. We are steadily chipping away those ledges and handholds in which Fukuyama takes comfort.

So, yes, we are sliding down the slippery slope. The question for the next chapter is whether we can belay, and then rebuild our political order.

The timing of ultimate breakdown is uncertain because political arrangements often last long past their sell-by date. People are cautious, and, per the Declaration of Independence, "Prudence, indeed, will dictate that Governments long established should not be changed for light and transient causes".

In a similar vein, economist Adam Smith answered a we-will-be-ruined prediction with a soothing, "Be assured... that there is a great deal of ruin in a nation". The aphorism is true of the United States, with its deep pool of human capital, respect for law, can-do ethic, and reserves of resilient optimism and religious faith. We take a lot of ruining.

We Americans are prone to our own style of "Whig history", which interprets the past as a steady growth in liberty and enlightenment that led to a present happy state and is trending toward an even more glorious future. In fact, the study of history is not an occupation for sissies, because many societies retrogress and disintegrate.

Historian Niall Ferguson recently instructed us that the assumption that civilizations decline gently is a myth. "A striking feature is the speed with which most of them collapsed, regardless of the cause", and, "If what we are risking is not decline but downright collapse, then the time frame may be even tighter than one election cycle."

Such pessimism is reinforced by the increasing complexity of civilization, which narrows margins for error. Everything is interconnected, so any breakdown cascades. The economic crisis since 2008 is a good example; everyone, especially so-called economic and investment experts, was caught flat-footed when moderate decline in the value of residential real estate in some markets cascaded into a large hit to the value of other assets in all markets, and a perilous flirtation with total melt-down.

We blithely assume that craziness caused by Big SIS and factional capture can be reversed before catastrophe happens, but we overlook the ratchet. Once something crazy gets through, it can wreak havoc while the legal and political systems are paralyzed. It would be unwise to assume that we are immune from something dire—my candidate is the crash of the electric grid, which is steadily deteriorating—or that we will be able forestall something dire even as it impends. The system has become too sclerotic.

During the economic crisis of the 1930s, 56 percent of the population lived in rural areas, and millions more had relatives there. People went back to the farm and self-sufficiency. Now, only 18 percent of us are rural, and only 2 percent of the workforce is in agriculture. Our collective back-to-the-land skills are laughable. Because agriculture is mechanized, even farmers are high tech now, and dependent on electricity and fuel. If any of our great networks collapses, or if Big SIS causes either economic stasis or a total collapse of political legitimacy, we will be in deep trouble very quickly.

The argument can be made that we will continue to limp along. What this overlooks is that we *have* been limping along; the structural flaws of Big SIS have been eroding the foundations of our polity for decades. Bad outcomes have been postponed by external events, such as the fall of the Soviet Empire, the information revolution, and the basic grit and competence of the American people. The time borrowed is up.

Indeed, Big SIS is moving toward a tipping point of instability, and the logic of tipping points dictates that deterioration will accelerate. As the Soviet Empire illustrated in 1989, as the current upheaval in the Mid-East is confirming, and as Ferguson predicts, basically unstable arrangements of all kinds tend to last longer than one would think possible, then collapse with great speed. If we are to regain our balance, we need substantial reforms in our political arrangements.

Crane Brinton's *Anatomy of Revolution*, first published in 1938, was on Professor Beer's reading list, and it warrants rereading. Brinton points to a dire consequence of a government's loss of legitimacy: in a crisis, people do not step up to defend it. The result of this passivity is that a surprisingly small group, if organized, can take control. Lenin said that the Bolsheviks did not seize power in 1917; they found it lying in the gutter and picked it up.

You can be sure that groups on the hard left, and maybe on the right, are familiar with this history and are working toward the day when American power will fall into the gutter. Those in the center have only a finite time in which to build a regime that reclaims legitimacy.

Chapter Five

An Alternative to Big SIS: Renewing the Republic

Fast-forward back to first principles

Contemporary political commentary constantly asserts that the system is in a crisis and that action is urgent. However, most of this writing is light on specific ideas for improvement. Proposals tend to be large and vague, as in "get control of spending" or "reform entitlements".

Well, yes. But such recommendations rather neglect an important point. They fail to explain how spending got out of control or why we have not already fixed it. They tell us to stop having the symptoms caused by Big SIS without suggesting lines of attack on Big SIS itself, or even noticing the existence of Big SIS.

This chapter takes the inquiry back a step. How might we reform our political order to bring factional destructiveness under control, and reduce factional depredations to manageable size? If the Founders could develop appropriate doctrines and mechanisms, why can't we?

Reformers in the conservative legal academy have some creative thoughts about Constitutional restoration and adaptation, discussed later in this chapter, but these are only a start. In general, we need to think not only about Constitutional doctrine but about the broader constitution. We need principles to guide our fundamental decisions, and a reasonably stable set of reformed institutions through which these principles can be applied over a sustained period.

The initial goal should be to recapture a collective recognition of the wisdom of the principles of the Old Republic:

- The conviction that laws must be for the general welfare, not for particular factions;

- Abhorrence of systemic corruption;

- Recognition that government cannot bear the prime responsibility for any area of society, except perhaps for the traditional public goods, even though it must often be an important facilitator.

Then, the task is to develop an institutional structure that buttresses these pillars of principle.

No single approach exists, and the possibilities are many. My suggested agenda is set forth at the end of this chapter, but readers will undoubtedly have their own ideas.

Before offering this agenda, it is useful to identify some constraints on our actions. One of the strengths of the

Founders was their ruthless realism about human nature and their refusal to lapse into wishing-will-make-it-so analysis. We should emulate this.

Not a democracy, a republic

The abstract word "democracy" is tossed around constantly, often as one side or another in a political battle accuses the other of being "undemocratic". Usually, the practical meaning of the term is left undefined.

Is "democracy" the rule by plebiscite on everything, with the ignorant and the knowing given equal weight? The mob rule of ochlocracy? The fascist tradition of one man, one vote, one time? Periodic elections of officials who then rule without restraint until the next one? Isocracy, in which all citizens have equal political power, or sortition, in which officeholders are chosen by lot? The New Left or Occupy Wall Street approach of rule by the iron-butted, who can sit through interminable meetings? The Leninist idea that democracy is the true will of the masses, as discerned by a vanguard that chooses a central committee that decides the nature of this true will?

It is irritating to note how often political pundits refer to something as democratic or undemocratic without defining the terms, and apparently without any awareness that a definition is necessary.

The problem with such open-ended discourse was pegged by Michael Greve of the American Enterprise Institute:

'Democracy' (full stop, period) is just a slogan. If it means an unstructured, undisciplined, exploitative interest group free-for-all—our politics, that is to say—it is an unpalatable alternative…. [I]f democracy means a structured, institutionally cabined and constitutionally disciplined form of government—a *republican* form of government…—it is emphatically worth having.

The Founders' vision of a democratic republic is the correct one. It is democratic in that sovereignty lies with the people, who use it to set up institutions that exercise power in specified ways, and who always retain the residual authority to revamp those institutions, but who are bound by the structures until they are formally changed. Democracy should not synonymous with *ad hocracy*.

Elections alone are not a sufficient condition for effective democracy. To return to Greve's point, they are part of a bigger package that includes limited government, respect and protection for minority views and populations, accountability of government officials, an independent judiciary, rule of law and the application of the law to the government and its officials, security of property rights, and protection of honest investment against either direct seizure or seizure by regulation.

Effective democracy also requires that these checks against capture by factions be effective even while the people are busy with their own lives and are not focusing on their government. Rational ignorance by the public about politics is an inevitable part of life, and the system must run smoothly nonetheless. It cannot work without delegating decisions to particular institutions that are not governed by popular vote in their day-to-day operations. A court of law is a fine example of such an institution. No one argues that formal criminal trials are nondemocratic; when criminal law is enforced by democratic means, it is called lynching. But nondemocratic, unbiased, fair, expert, and nonpolitical tribunals are a vital component of any political society that aspires to be a democracy.

A working democratic republic also requires a large private civil society and a primarily free-market economy, both insulated from special-interest-dominated government meddling. Otherwise, private institutions will inevitably turn into Little SISes. The mortgage companies, Fannie

Mae and Freddie Mac, are poster children. They evolved from worthy institutions designed to smooth out the mortgage market into corrupt entities devoted to enriching politicians and their friends and over-promoting home ownership for the benefit of special interests.

The recent fate of General Motors (*aka* Government Motors) is also illustrative, as within a year of its takeover by government its business decisions became dependent on the demands of the union and True Green supporters of the current administration.

When someone criticizes any of these insulated-from-government private institutions as undemocratic, the answer should be, "Exactly! That is its strength!" The genius of a republic is its blend of limited government and autonomous private institutions that most emphatically *do not* mimic the government's response to special-interest pressures.

The positive use of self-interest

Another truth is that Big SIS did not triumph because of irrationality. Rather, the present system is the accretion of decisions by people acting rationally within the circumstances in which they found themselves.

Once the old taboos on special-interest favoritism were broken and Big SIS got rolling, it was inevitable that citizens would organize to obtain and then defend gains, and to fend off attacks from other interests. It was equally inevitable that others would organize to demand comparable treatment and that the political system would react by adding, but never subtracting, streams of benefits.

Everyone feels righteous, too, because they believe the propaganda of their chosen champions. Every subsidy quickly turns into an entitlement. The recipients believe themselves to be deserving. It is those other greedy bastards who are breaking the nation.

The result is that it is rational for voters to disapprove of Congress' pork-barrel addiction in general while wanting their own representatives to bring home the bacon in particular. It is consistent for a congressman to rail against subsidies in general on the floor and then fight for particular earmarks in committee. It makes sense for a senior to say he wants the government to keep its hands off his Medicare.

In addition, no interest would gain if it alone were stricken by an attack of public spirit. That would only leave more for the other interests. One may deplore the current system and wish it were different, but in the short term, no good comes of withdrawing one's cattle from an overgrazed pasture when others will respond by enlarging their herds rather than by exercising reciprocal restraint. A governor who turns down federal money for a bridge to nowhere knows that the money will not be returned to the taxpayers; it will be spent on some equally worthless project in a different state.

So the AARP runs its ads urging budgetary responsibility—but not at the cost of a dime of seniors' benefits. Every other interest does the same.

This rationality makes the system very stubborn. The nation has a large store of republican virtue, but it erodes as people realize that others are waiting in line to take advantage if they lapse into a sense of public responsibility. In the world of Washington influence peddling, an exhibition of civic virtue by anyone is regarded as an amusing character flaw that can be exploited for the benefit of one's own clients.

Understanding the nature of the system does not necessarily lead to reform. Mancur Olson died early, before he could devote serious thought to how a society could escape the downward spiral of Big SIS. The little he wrote was mostly pessimistic, but he suggested that once people understood the dynamics of special interests, they would be better able to resist them.

So far, this hope has not worked out. Instead, it is the interests that have grasped the dynamics of collective action and Big SIS and learned to better take advantage of them. The interests also seem to understand the remorseless logic of "the last period problem", which dictates that you should respond to a crisis by redoubling your efforts to loot the system before it breaks down.

However, there is a sunnier counter-consideration. An advantage of the special interests is that rational ignorance is the normal state of the public, while rational knowledge is the normal state of the interests.

As crisis impends, public ignorance becomes less rational, so the public has an incentive to become better informed. As citizen groups achieve parity of knowledge, they will be better able to counter special-interest propaganda and legerdemain. Olson's hope that knowledge will foster reform might become reality.

Another powerful factor on the positive side of the ledger is that narrow short-term self-interest is not the only kind. A more intelligent self-interest takes a long-term view.

From this perspective, any fool can see that Big SIS cannot continue indefinitely and that collapse and stasis benefit no one. Most of us would benefit from scrapping Big SIS, particularly because of the vast increases in productivity and wealth that would result from freeing up resources for better uses. Even those who think they would lose would probably wind up better off in the not-too-distant future.

A crucial point is that renewing the republic does not require us to renounce self-interest. No sermons are needed on how we must all work together and abandon our selfish goals and become imbued with a new spirit of cooperation and generosity. This is good, because wishing for reform of basic human nature is not a winning course. In another of the Founders' famous lines, *from Federalist No 51*: "If men were angels, no government would be necessary. If angels were to govern men, neither external nor internal controls on government would be necessary."

So we must accept the Founders' insight that faction is unavoidable and cannot be eradicated. Besides, the power of self-interest will always make itself felt. If the government prevents people from competing to be better producers, then in their own self-interest they will compete to be more pathetic victims and compassion traps will multiply, or they will compete for government office. The power motive is as strong as the profit motive and is usually more destructive.

We cannot even imagine a society that is not divided into groups and interests, except perhaps a Marxist paradise, and we all know how that idea turned out.

Nor would eradicating faction be a good thing. It is a vital source of energy, and Lincoln's comment that the patent system adds "the fuel of interest to the fire of genius" can be expanded. We rely on interest to fuel a market-based economic system and should appreciate its role in the political system. This essay has said many nasty things about special interests, but, properly constrained and channeled, they are prodigious generators of information and action.

Fortunately, rejection of self-interest is not necessary for people to recognize the need to reform our political institutions. They need only realize that establishing a government of unending competition for special-interest favors is a negative-sum game, with far more losers than winners, and it results in the overall destruction of productivity. This recognition is called common sense.

The lesson is that we need not reject self-interest. We can embrace it avidly, only it should be of the intelligent, long-term variety, not a short-sighted grab-a-subsidy-today mentality.

Repeat over and over: "a collective action problem"

The basic nature of our dilemma is called "a collective action problem". In all societies, there is a tension between the desire of each individual or faction to obtain special advantages and exploit others and the common interest of all in establishing general rules that prevent exploitation of anyone by anyone. For a society to work, people must have mechanisms for making bargains in which all agree to reject temptations to yield to short-term greed, in return for which they receive protection from the greed of others, so that all may do better in the long term.

As previous chapters have touched upon, collective action problems often arise in the context of a commons—a natural resource such as a pasture, hunting ground, fishing area, water source, or oil field, where rampant exploitation will deplete the resource. The logic of the situation is that every individual has an incentive to take the maximum before others grab it.

Societies solve problem of "the commons" all the time. They establish quotas; they pool interests into a corporation or cooperative and install a single manager who divides the returns according to prior agreement; they establish social norms and ostracize violators; they invent mechanisms of property rights. "The commons" is the subject of a large and interesting theoretical and historical literature.

At a more general level, addressing collective action dilemmas is the fundamental point of creating a government. A vital part of a successful democratic republic is that the institutions solve the collective-action problems. They must guarantee that all will exercise restraint in pursuit of self-interest, and they must also have built-in protections against efforts by people to corrupt them in individual cases.

The term "collective action" had not been invented when *The Federalist* papers were written, but their discussion of factions is about solving the collective-action issues inherent in organizing a society. The Founders achieved this by establishing a variety of institutions, which were then set to watch each other. Now, their structure has broken down, so we need to either repair the old ones or create some new ones that will check the always-watchful appetites of factions.

In concept, understanding the importance of such institutions is no more complicated than analyzing the possible responses to a natural resources commons. A simple illustration is the use of an escrow agent to buy a house. From a totally selfish standpoint, the seller would like to obtain the cash and then renege on transferring the deed, while the buyer wants to get the deed and then bounce the check. The solution is the escrow agent, instructed by both parties to collect both the deed and the money and then pass them on to the appropriate parties.

One way to understand Big SIS is to realize that we fired the escrow agents, and so we have condemned ourselves to lawless collisions of raw self-interest.

In normal times, an effort to get the public to recognize that our problems are due to failures of the institutions that solve collective action problems would have difficulty penetrating the noise of short-term propaganda. In a time of crisis, however, when the public is seeking information and understanding, the effort has a chance of succeeding. Defining the issues properly would be a giant step toward reform.

The reform effort is helped by another development that belongs on the plus side of the ledger—the growth of the Internet, which makes communication, interaction, and organization cheaper and easier.

Granted, the special interests use these tools, too, but these were already well-organized under the old, expensive technologies. The new modes narrow the advantage of the zombies over the citizens, to the advantage of the citizens. The new media also allow reformers to avoid the old mainstream media, which has long been one of the great pillars of Big SIS.

The fluidity of the new communications helps in another way. An organized special interest is usually a hierarchical organization. Anyone who has sat in the councils of large associations knows how stodgy and slow these are. They cannot risk offending the dumbest executive of any of their members, and there are many dumb executives in the world. Citizens' organizations can be agile and quick to seize opportunity. They need not paralyze themselves waiting for approval from higher up, they can flow around stupidity rather than be dominated by it, and they have proven that they can raise money efficiently. They can be law professor Glenn Reynolds' *Army of Davids*.

An immediate agenda

Specifically, though, what should we do immediately, starting next Monday morning? Here is a list.

Education and advocacy

Step 1 is education and advocacy. People who care about the future of the nation should educate others on the nature of the problem. Identifying it as the need to solve issues of collective action taps into a very useful body of thought by some excellent thinkers. Names like Mancur Olson and Jonathan Rauch should be familiar to everyone in the debate.

As part of the effort, everyone who values the republic should also emphasize the basic values of the Old Republic—that laws should serve the general welfare, not some faction; that systemic corruption is evil, and the nineteenth-century images of rot and putrescence were on the mark; and that government should not be regarded as responsible for major societal systems but only as a participant that has some power and a responsibility to make them work better.

When some politician talks of "targeted tax cuts" or "temporary support" or "innovation plans" or of a minor easing of stupid regulations or of "mend don't end" some broken program, or when he or she uses some other buzzword of the day, the response should be laughter. No one should take this nonsense seriously—the speaker doesn't—because it is a plea for whatever interest is supporting the politician this time, a ploy designed to lure the public back into its sleep of rational ignorance, or both.

Government rarely ends a program, almost nothing is temporary, and little is repaired. Minor changes are designed to cool the public temper while maintaining the status quo, and the only targets hit by specialized tax breaks are the contribution levels desired by the politicians' fund-raisers.

The point must be made constantly that Big SIS lacks political legitimacy and that it cannot be allowed to continue.

Elections

Step 2 is politics and elections. We must elect a president and legislators who see the problems and are determined to solve them. They must endorse the ideas of tax reform, of an end to the 2000+ subsidies, and of skepticism that the government is capable of running much of anything.

Slaughter the sacred cows

Once we elect officials dedicated to reform, we should think big about step 3. We should point toward a grand tax-reform bill, a big slaughter-the-subsidies bill, and serious reform of Social Security, Medicare, and Medicaid.

It would be appropriate to pass such big reform bills on August 4 of some year in the near future. August 4, 1789, was, as a book title says, *The Night the Old Regime Ended* during the French Revolution. The nobility and clergy of France engaged in an orgy of renunciation of old feudal rights, privileges, and titles. At the end of the evening, the nation was transformed.

The French experience teaches two lessons. One is that such astounding things can indeed happen. The other is that it is better not to leave them until too late; despite the renunciation, many of those aristocrats went to the guillotine or exile in 1793.

It is important to note the improbability of reforming Big SIS bit-by-bit. The logic of special-interest knowledge and public ignorance will always stall and then abort piecemeal reforms. We need big reforms at a time when the public is rationally aware.

Pressure your own special-interest representatives

Step 4 is for each of us to pressure our own special-interest groups to be part of the solution. I do not belong to the AARP (formerly the American Association of Retired Persons), primarily because its greed on behalf of its clients and its reckless disregard for their grandchildren annoys me. Its members need to pressure the organization to change its ways.

My level of optimism will take an uptick the day I see an AARP ad that says: "Social Security and Medicare must be reformed, and we know we will take a hit, but we are willing to do our part as long as others do too." And I will get positively euphoric when the Natural Resources Defense

Council (NRDC) and the National Wildlife Federation (NWF) say, "We know that cheap energy is the foundation of civilization, and we are determined to find reasonable compromises that reflect the needs of both energy production and environmental protection."

As noted earlier, the incentive structures work against this, and it would take courage, so some of the biggest players should step up. It would be particularly useful for us seniors to take the lead, as the present structure subsidizes us at the expense of those who are both younger and poorer than seniors as a group.

Businesses and producers must get in the right game

Step 5 is that businesses and producers must step up to their public responsibilities.

These entities have lost the habit of defending the free market and the general welfare in favor of pursuing their own short-term special interests. In the end, this is a mug's game because it is negative for the overall economy, most of the participants will lose, and the intermediaries will siphon off the profits anyway. So these institutions must recognize their own true interests and eliminate their Washington-fostered false consciousness.

Businesses and producers must also realize that pursuit of the special interest game has compromised their credibility when they seek laws that are indeed useful and necessary to make the economic system work smoothly. As noted in chapter 4, there is too much noise in the system, and much of it is generated by institutions whose real overwhelming interest should be in promoting efficiency-enhancing rules.

Closely connected to this loss of credibility: corporate headquarters should reclaim control of their government affairs strategies from their Washington offices and representatives. These agents have sets of interests that are different from and in many ways opposed to the interests of their principals.

Reclaim respect for civic virtue

Step 6 is directed at the Washington government affairs staffs and firms.

It is no accident that young lawyers are not a bunch of happy campers. Providing information to Congress and agencies, protecting the clients against predation, and devising legislation that makes society and the market run smoothly is an honorable and necessary occupation. Being a mercenary willing to use any means to seek favors and advantage on behalf of anyone who walks in the door is not, nor is being an all-out defender of a system that depends on such favoritism.

Only total cynics can enjoy such an existence, and that is not a good mental or spiritual state in which to live. The young need to join the reform movement precisely so that they can lead more fulfilling lives. They should want a structure that limits what the clients can ask of them, one that explicitly and proudly recognizes their obligations to maintain the integrity of the republic.

This advice is emphatically not limited to the representatives of business. The representatives of the *soi disant* "public interest" are every bit as ruthless, and maybe more so.

Similarly, citizen activists and other forces of light must recognize the potential for honor in congressional staffs and young bureaucrats. Most come to Washington with good intentions. Then, after a few years in the sausage factory, they ecome acculturated to the values of the clients and demands of the political system. An example is my story in the Introduction about transit subsidies; had I stayed at the Department of Housing and Urban Development, within a couple of years I would have been puzzled by any suggestion that I might have an obligation to the taxpayers rather than to the clients of HUD.

The young government workers then grow cynical and decide there is no such thing as good anyway, so they give up and settle for doing well by going into lobbying. Before they are captured, there is potential for reform.

Control the Regulatory State

Step 7 is that the Regulatory State must be brought under supervision. This could involve giving sharper teeth to the Office of Management and Budget, or giving the Congressional Budget Office the responsibility for conducting the benefit/cost analyses. The pending Regulations from the Executive in Need of Scrutiny (REINS) Act would require that regulations with $100 million in impact be approved as laws.

I vote for all three ideas.

REINS might have the added benefit of forcing Congress to revisit some basic agency organic acts that compel results that Congressmen would be reluctant to endorse if they were held accountable. Dodd-Frank, ObamaCare, the Clean Air Act, and the Endangered Species Act are particular examples, but the list is long.

Legal education and reform

Step 8: the legal profession is in need of serious intellectual reform. Reading contemporary opinions on government power is like making an archaeological dig into the intellectual ruins of the political thinking of the 1930s, if not the 1910s. Supreme Court cases, especially, are striking in that the Court is unfamiliar with such terms as "special interest state", "collective action", and "Public Choice" when its main business should consist of dealing with the issues wrapped up in these concepts.

Judges should jettison their Progressive Era assumptions that bureaucrats are all disinterested experts improving the lot of us plebeians. Public Choice theory, which recognizes that government employees are as filled with self-interest as anyone else, and that they protect the interests of themselves and their clients, would be a more tenable starting point.

"Lawyers should get smarter" is not by itself practical advice, but some specific recommendations are already under exploration in the conservative wing of the legal academy.

Constitutional law went seriously astray in the Supreme Court's crabbed interpretation of the Fourteenth Amendment's Privileges and Immunities Clause during the 1870s. This cannot be written off as old error that is now frozen by the doctrine of *stare decisis* (which holds that, for the sake of stability and predictability, past decisions should not be revisited) because the mistake cascaded, distorting subsequent jurisprudence about the Commerce Clause and government power generally. A confession of error and acknowledgment that many subsequent decisions were actually P&I in disguise could bear healthy Constitutional fruit in the future, even though the immediate legal upheaval would indeed be large.

Other areas in which the conservative legal academy is pushing intellectual reform include a rationalization of the law governing the taking of private property for public use, which has drifted into incoherence, and a renewed dedication to the field called "economic liberties"—the idea that the right to make a living is as fundamental as rights of speech and religion. The doctrine of substantive due process, which holds that the Constitution imposes substantive as well as procedural limits on the government, needs to be revived in the context of economic regulation and its contours debated.

Courts could also revive the concept of equal protection as a yardstick for assessing legislation. During the nineteenth century, courts thought it logical to insist that legislation be general as part of their overall dedication to the general welfare. This check on special-interest abuses disappeared when they agreed that the government needed a free hand to micromanage economic affairs, because micromanagement requires fine distinctions among categories of citizens, distinctions which then lend themselves to favoritism and abuse.

Since then, the government has proven its total inability to manage anything, so its need for the untrammeled power required for micromanagement should be rejected. Reasonable generality in legislation is absolutely necessary to liberty.

If judges are reluctant to accept responsibility for assessing the rationality of economic legislation, they should at least be able to examine its generality. This is especially true considering that in other contexts, such as discrimination, courts feel competent to assess the reasonableness of distinctions drawn by legislatures.

Another interesting possibility floating around the academy and the political system is worth a close look. The Supreme Court turned the Ninth and Tenth Amendments to the Constitution into dead letters. Interest in both, especially the Tenth, is reviving, especially in states angry at federal intrusions.

Yet another idea concerns the direct election of senators. Until the Constitution was amended in 1917, each state decided its own selection process. In the nineteenth century, state legislators usually did the job. Direct election radically changed the relationship between state and federal governments by ending a senator's role as a representative of his or her state government in Washington, and it is far from clear that this was a good idea. Return to the old system seems unlikely, but debating the issue would improve understanding of contemporary politics.

As a historical matter, our society relied upon the legal system and the courts to enforce the collective action bargains necessary to make the society run. The courts got out of that business in the 1930s, and results have not been pretty. Perhaps, as the judges claim, they will not be very competent at the job, but they would be better than the nothing that we have now.

In the longer term, new institutions can be invented. The private sector, especially the technology industry, is ingenious at creating institutions directed at solving collective action problems, as illustrated by the history of standard-setting organizations and other contract-based entities. Designers of government could profit from their example.

Those of us who want to rejuvenate legal doctrines and institutions to better protect our economic liberties against factional depredations are often accused of wanting to return to the nineteenth century.

This accusation is the reverse of the truth. We want to learn from the experience of the twentieth century, which shows that removing all checks on government power does not result in wise rule by disinterested mandarins. It produces, in Michael Greve's words, "an unstructured, undisciplined, exploitive interest group free-for-all".

These hard lessons should spur the legal profession to create mechanisms better adapted to the realities of the twenty-first century. It is our critics who refuse to recognize that law must evolve in the light of experience, as they cling to the failed political and legal dogmas of the Progressive Era, the New Deal, and the Great Society. They emulate the royal House of Bourbon after the French

Revolution: "They have learned nothing and forgotten nothing."

Real campaign finance reform

Step 9 is to eliminate most campaign finance laws except disclosure requirements, and perhaps the ban on direct corporate contributions to candidates. The effort to ban nefarious influence turns legislators into beggars and extortionists who must seek money from all special interests, creates overwhelming advantages for candidates who are rich, dynastic, or celebrated, and excludes the public spirited in favor of the corrupt.

The so-called reforms also advantage those, such as public employee unions and Hollywood entertainers, who can provide unregulated services. They have neutered the political parties as potential guardians of the republic and limited their ability to help legislators stand against SIS pressure; in addition, they have turned the Democrats in particular into a coalition of looters lacking any philosophy of proper government.

Efforts to restrict campaign finance still further are in fact efforts to enhance, not diminish, the power of factions.

Health care

Step 10: an essential change to promote the long-term health of Americans, both fiscal and physical, is to reform the medical payments system. The current value of the government's future obligations for these payments is about $58 trillion, and the chances that the system will be viable are zero. We can land hard, or we can land soft.

Reforming medical care payments should not be a hard problem. The government should sever insurance from employment by changing the tax laws to eliminate the break for employer-provided insurance, either by taxing the value of the employer contribution or exempting the costs of private insurance. It should allow health insurers to cross state lines so as to create more competition. It should eliminate coverage mandates, and thereby allow people to assess their own best interests, such as the purchase of high-deductible catastrophe insurance combined with self-funding of medical routine. A safety net is needed for the poor and disabled, but this should be implemented with mechanisms to minimize compassion traps.

Above all, no health care reform can work if it starts from the premise enunciated in the DC Circuit's opinion in *Susan Seven-Sky* that health care is a "national problem" that requires a Congress free to "forge national solutions". Health care is a service, a product, and a system that requires freedom from the palsied hand of Big SIS, not subjection to it.

Back to the future on nominating presidential candidates

Step 11: Perhaps the most important escrow agents fired were the political parties, which got "reformed" in the turmoil of the 1960s and 1970s.

Expensive presidential primaries determined by television ads, two-minute debate segments, late-night comedy shows, boots-on-the-ground public employee unions, fund-raising clout, and caucus trickery are a poor substitute for a national conclave of party activist intermediaries who are rationally knowledgeable about the interests and candidates.

We should bring back the old system of nominating presidential candidates. The parties should act as gate-keepers for the system; the electorate at large, rationally ignorant as always (and properly so), should choose from a menu put together by the intermediaries.

Coda

Looking back over this essay as a whole, and despite the gloom at the end of chapter 4, we should be at least cautiously optimistic.

The problems created by Big SIS are intractable in the normal course of politics-as-usual. But events are jolting us out of this rut and opening up new possibilities.

Big SIS depends on the momentum created by people making decisions on the basis of short-term self-interest. In the larger view, people are rational enough to understand that long-term interest trumps short-term, and to find ways to shift the balance. We are at a point of constitutional crisis, and this is all to the good. Only in such times does the public pay enough attention to assert its true long-term interest.

Besides, while the workaday pressures of a society may depend on self-interest, the great tides of history are moral and spiritual, and these can sweep away many structures once thought solid. Pure self-interest cannot explain the politics of the Revolutionary Era, the Civil War, the Progressive Age, the New Deal, the Civil Rights Revolution, or the Environmental Movement. To understand those tidal forces, you must understand the great moral strength of American civilization.

As the Tea Party movement shows, our classic ability for justified moral outrage is asserting itself again. So, hopefully, future historians will refer to the Renaissance of the early twenty-first century, when the American Republic renewed itself by recovering its old and tested values and adapting them to the age of high-tech, and regained its legitimacy.

This hope is ambitious but not unrealistic. It should be within our grasp. If we fail and Big SIS continues its downward spiral, a crisis will eventually occur, and power will wind up lying in the gutter. Who picks it up and what they do with it—that will be a topic for some future Professor Beer teaching a course on political legitimacy a couple of hundred years from now, perhaps at Beijing University.

Even more famous than the quote with which I began this essay—"A Republic, if you can keep it"—is another Benjamin Franklin quotation. As the delegates to the Constitutional Convention in 1787 were signing the document, Franklin pointed to the image of the sun on the chair of the convention president and said: "I have often... in the course of this session...looked at that...without being able to tell whether it was rising or setting; but now at length I have the happiness to know that it is a rising and not a setting sun."

We can prove that he is still right.

Endnotes

The endnotes provide sources for quotations and other specific points. Because this book is intended primarily as an e-book, in which page numbers are not fixed, the titles of the sections and subsections of the book are repeated to orient the reader, except when no notes refer to the subdivision. Each note is also introduced by a few words to establish its context.

The references section that follows these endnotes provides complete information on the books and articles used, so the endnotes list only the last name of the author, an abbreviated title, and the page number, where relevant. A few notes stand alone, without a connection to the references—obvious websites, Web quotation directories, and such.

Chapter One: Introduction to Big SIS

"A Republic, if you can keep it"

Franklin quotation: Bartleby.com. www.bartleby.com/73/1593.html

Definition of faction: *Federalist No. 10.*

Olson's three books are *The Logic of Collective Action; The Rise and Decline of Nations; Power and Prosperity.*

"A dreadful image of a spreading rot"

Systemic corruption: Wallis, *Systemic Corruption.*

Banning quotation: Banning, *Jeffersonian Persuasion*, p.47. (The definition of systemic corruption is from Wallis.)

Appropriations earmarks: Taxpayers for Common Sense, *Earmarks.*

Cash for Clunkers: Jacoby, *Clunker Q & A.*

Rural Development vote: DeMint, *We're Still Not Cutting.*

"Government's power...": Rauch, *Democlerosis*, p.17.

Madison's statement on the inevitability of faction: *Federalist No. 10.*

"Fuel of interest": Lincoln, *Second Lecture on Discoveries and Inventions.*

Barrier islands: Hanna, *Green Scissors.*

Crash: Olson, *Power and Prosperity*, pp.98, 167. The Napoleonic invasion point is in Acemoglu, *The Consequences of Radical Reform.*

"The claim of a government to...obedience and loyalty"

"Legendary": Grimes, *Samuel H. Beer, Authority on British Government, Dies at 97.*

Beer's definition of political legitimacy: Beer, *To Make a Nation*, p.343.

Preview of this book and what to do next Monday morning

Churchill used the "sunlit uplands" phrase in his most famous speech to Parliament, usually called *Their Finest Hour.*

Chapter Two: How We Got Here: The Rise of Big SIS

"Some common impulse of passion, or of interest"

Samuel's warning: *The Bible*, King James version, 1 Samuel 8.
William the Conqueror: Thomas Paine, *Common Sense* (1776).
Madison on faction: *Federalist No. 10.*
Corruption: Wallis, *Concept of Systematic Corruption*, pp.25, 33.
East India Company: Kopel, *British Gun Control*; Carp, *Defiance of the Patriots.*
Judge Kozinski on the Second Amendment: The statement is in his 2003 dissent from the Order Denying Petition for Rehearing En Banc in *Silveira v Lockyer*, 312 F.3d 1052 (2002).
Defense in depth: Voegeli, *Never Enough*, p.64.
Hughes quotation: Keller, *America's Three Regimes*, p.37.
Scalia quotation: Scalia, *Considering the Role of Judges Under the Constitution of the United States* (Oct. 5, 2011).

The Constitution, the constitution, and political legitimacy

Definition of "regime": Tushnet, *The New Constitutional Order*, p.1.
Political legitimacy: Beer, *To Make a Nation*, p.343.
Wickard v. Filburn, 317 U.S. 111 (1942); *United States v. Carolene Products*, 304 U.S. 144 (1938).
Law is an ass: Charles Dickens, *Oliver Twist (1838)*, p.489.
Kelo: *Kelo v. City of New London*, 545 U.S. 469 (2005).

State redevelopment agencies: Greenhut, *California's Secret Government.*

Rudyard Kipling, *Norman and Saxon* (1911).

"Fear of corruption verging on paranoia": the Old Republic

Fear of corruption: Wallis, *Constitutions, Corporations, and Corruption,* p.29, quoting Lance Banning, *The Jeffersonian Persuasion,* p.47.

Wisconsin: Ranney, *Making of the Wisconsin Constitution.*

North Carolina: Kickler, *North Carolina History Project.*

State courts and due process: R. Williams, *Substantive Due Process Clause,* p.465.

$450 million: Wallis, *Concept of Systemic Corruption,* p.44.

109-page survey: Gillman, *The Constitution Besieged,* pp.106–10.

20 of 37 states: R. Williams, *Substantive Due Process Clause,* p.469.

Taxing power: Dauber, *The Sympathetic State,* p.52–53.

Functions of government: *Kelly v. Pittsburgh,* 104 U.S. 78 (1881).

Disaster relief: Dauber, *The Sympathetic State,* pp.9–10.

Ohio: Thies, *American Railroad Network,* p.241.

Clay speech: Clay, *In Defense of the American System.*

The Old Republic in the Post-Civil War Era

Federal revenues: *U.S. Government Taxes and Revenue Since 1900.*

Municipal bond cases: Greve, *Commerce, Competition, and the Court.*

Minorities and local animus: D. Bernstein, *Lochner, Parity, and the Chinese Laundry Cases.*

Legal and political approaches to the general welfare and corruption issues: The analysis is drawn from the works of Barry Cushman, Howard Gillman, David Bernstein, Richard Epstein, and John Eastman listed in the References section. They do not always agree with each other, and none is responsible for my conclusions. It should hardly be necessary to caution that this is a broad and complex topic, here greatly simplified.

Garbage and horses: Melosi, *Garbage in the Cities.*

"The police power": R. Epstein, *How Progressives Rewrote the Constitution.*

The need for law

Huntington's letters: Quoted in Lewis, *The People or the Railroads?*"

Chicago aldermen: Ginger, *Altgeld's America.*

For discussion of the connections between nineteenth-century railroads and current networks: DeLong, *Avoiding a Tech Train Wreck.*

Union Pacific financing: Crawford, *The Credit Mobilier of America*; Thies, *The American Railroad Network*; Commissioner of the U.S. General Land Office, Report. For a more condemnatory view, see Ripley, *Railroad Construction Finance.*

Twentieth/twenty-first–century corruption: David Goldman, *Republicans, Democrats and Wall Street Fraud.*

Networks, platforms, and the nationalization of industry

Stranded horses: Livermore, *My Story of the War*, p.315.

Lifespan of NYC horse: Melosi, *Garbage in the Cities*, p.21.

Rising pay: R. Epstein, *How Progressives Rewrote the Constitution*, p.5.

Quote on rising living standards and inequality of bargaining power: D. Bernstein, *Lochner, Parity, and the Chinese Laundry Cases*, p.213.

Gillman: Gillman, *Regime Politics*.

Sherman quote: Miller, *Great Debates in American History*, Vol. 11, p.39.

Cost of lighting: Folsom, *John D. Rockefeller and the Oil Industry*.

Tarbell: A. Epstein, *Vindicating Capitalism*; Henderson, *Of Price and Men*.

Cordage trust: Alfred Chandler, *The Visible Hand*.

Councils and self-interest: Goldberg, *Liberal Fascism*, pp. 292–94.

The Old Republic as of 1929: battered but upright

Harding quotation: *TeachingAmericanHistory.org.* www.teachingamericanhistory.org/library/index.asp?document=954

Definition of conservatism: Goldberg, *Liberal Fascism*, pp. 129–30.

Vote totals in 1920: Wikipedia.

The Great Depression, the New Deal, and the onrush of Big SIS

Herbert Hoover: Horwitz, *Herbert Hoover*.

Experimentation: F. D. Roosevelt, *Speech at Oglethorpe University*.

"Don't know what New Deal is": The statement was made by economist Alvin Hansen, and is one of the stock quotations used by skeptics of the New Deal. See Alan Brinkley, *The New Deal and the Idea of the State*.

Effect of a gold clause on a lease: see *216 Jamaica Ave LLC v. Playhouse Reality Co.*, (Sixth Cir. Aug 2008).

"For two years": Dunn, *Death by Liberalism*, p.8.

Effect of New Deal on securities industry: Mahoney, *The Political Economy of the Securities Act of 1933.*

Barry Cushman: Polling data is at Cushman, *Mr. Dooley and Mr. Gallup.* The broader point is covered in the series of articles by Cushman listed in the References section.

Moley quotation: Goldberg, *Liberal Fascism*, p.129.

Cover stories: S. Williams, *Transitions.*

Interest Group Liberalism: Lowi, *The End of Liberalism.*

Civil Rights

King quotation: Martin Luther King, Jr., *Letter from Birmingham Jail.*

"Distressing" Supreme Court decisions: *Slaughter-House Cases*, 83 U.S. 36 (1873) & *United States v. Cruikshank*, 92 U.S. 542 (1875).

Statistics on lynching: Univ. Missouri-Kansas City Law School: *Lynching in America: Statistics, Information, Images.*

No African Americans at 1913 Gettysburg Reunion: Foner, *Book Review of David W. Blight.*

Clemenceau quotation: Clemenceau, *American Reconstruction*, pp.299–300.

Environmentalism

Effect of Carson's book: Norhaus & Shellenberger, *Break Through*, p.130.

Positive feedback

Number of lobbyists: *Open Secrets*; Rauch, *Government's End*, p.43.

AARP members: AARP website. AFSCM members: AFSCM website. NRDC members: NRDC website.

"A chain reaction": Rauch, *Government's End*, p.121.

"Raining federal soup": Reynolds, *Is Democracy Like Sex?* p.1653

"Bootleggers and Baptists": Yandle, *Bootleggers and Baptists.*

Chapter Three: Where We Are: Big SIS Today

Mapping the territory

Brinton: Brinton, *The Anatomy of Revolution, pp. 33–34.*

Following the money

<u>Direct expenditures</u>

Levels of government spending: usgovernmentspending. com.

Government employees: Murray, *Stealing You Blind*, p.20.

Subsidy programs: Edwards, *Federal Aid-to-State Programs;* See also U.S. Government, *Catalog of Federal Domestic Assistance.*

<u>Tax expenditures (special tax breaks) and collection costs</u>

Tax Expenditures: See OMB, *Analytical Perspectives, Budget of the Unites States Government, Fiscal Year 2012,* Ch. 17 & U.S. Congress, Joint Committee on Taxation, Background Information on Tax Expenditure Analysis.

Effect of tax breaks: Kaiser, *So Damn Much Money.*

CCH: CCH website.

Compliance time: National Taxpayer Advocate, *2010 Annual Report.*

Compliance costs: Laffer, *Economic Burden.*

<u>Loans, guarantees, and manipulation of interest rates.</u>

Federal financial guarantees: Walter & Weinberg, *How Large?*; Malysheva & Walter, *How Large;* Kane, *Measuring Systemic Risk.*

Student loans: Cauchon, *Student loans outstanding.*
Catalogue: *Catalogue of Federal Domestic Assistance.*

Regulatory costs

Number of federal agencies: GPO, *Government Manual,*
   Appendix C. See also *USA.gov.*
California agencies: Fierce Reason, *California's Unsustainable*
   Existence.
Information on regulations: Crews, *Ten Thousand*
   Commandments.

Laws

Number of federal criminal laws: Baker, *Revisiting the*
   Explosive Growth of Federal Crimes.
Everyone violates law: Silverglate, *Three Felonies a Day.*
DOJ hiring: PJ Media, *Every Single One.*
Climate change: *When the Police Knock on Your Door.*
Plaintiffs' tort bar: Manhattan Institute, *Trial Lawyers Inc.:*
   Attorneys General (2011).
Antitrust: DeLong, *The New Trustbusters.*
Overlawyered: www.overlawyered.com

Adding it up

Cato and budget cuts: Edwards, *Downsizing the Federal*
   Government.
"Hard core of fat": Rough paraphrase of personal
   recollection.
Public school Salaries: Richwine & Biggs, *Assessing the*
   Compensation.
Universal Service Fund: Website of the Universal Service
   Administration Company. http://www.universalservice.
   org/about/universal-service.

Whenever there is a danger: Trzupek, *Regulators Gone Wild.*

10 lobbying firms: Lavelle & Lewis, *Climate lobbying dominated by 10 firms.*

Fees on retirement accounts: Butler, *Hidden Fees in 401(k) Plans;*

Hutcheson, *Are Hidden Fees Undermining Employment Retirement Income Security?*

Transfer to the elderly: Hinderaker, *The Purpose of Government.*

Distorting other institutions

Rauch quotation: Rauch, *Government's End,* p.119.

Edifice complex: Parkinson talked about the phenomenon in Chapter 8 of *Parkinson's Law,* but he did not use the phrase "edifice complex" in that book. See the excerpt at www.brianmicklethwait.com/index.php/weblog/ professor_c_northcote_parkinson_on_the_edifice_ complex/. A Web search reveals that his name is firmly linked with the term.

Income tax industry: Keating, *A Taxing Trend.*

Taibbi, *Wall Street Isn't Winning—It's Cheating.*

Financial columnist: Brown, *Dear Jamie Dimon.*

Capital/labor: Orzag, *As Kaldor's Facts Fall.*

Growth in lawyers/advocacy groups: Rauch, *Government's End,* p.120.

"This isn't fair dealing"

Defense earmarks: Taxpayers for Common Sense website.

Green jobs: Furchtgott-Roth, *Obama's Green-Energy Jobs Lie.*

Chipotle: *Antoninetti v. Chipotle Mexican Grill,* U.S. Court of Appeals for the Ninth Circuit (July 26, 2010).

SOX: AEI, *Is Sarbanes-Oxley Impairing Corporate Risk-Taking?*

Rural California: Greenhut, *Rural rebellion brewing.*

Health care: Antos, *Still No Good News for ObamaCare.*

Alabama meeting: McElroy, *I'm just quitting.*

Corporate executive: Tigerhawk, *Occupy this.*

Energy points: Taken from numerous news stories.

Video game industry: Kocieniewski, *Rich Tax Breaks Bolster Makers of Video Games.*

Kaiser statement: DeMint, *Venture socialism.*

FWS: Taken from numerous news sources.

Chain link fence: McArdle, *'Historic' Preservation.*

Subsidies to Brazil & generally: Grunwald, *Why the U.S. Is Also Giving Brazilians Farm Subsidies;* Grunwald, *The Farm Bill Stalls.*

Subsidies generally: Environmental Working Group, *2011 Farm Subsidy Data Base.*

IRS liens: National Taxpayer Advocate, *2010 Annual Report,* p.10.

CO2: Simmons, *EPA's Absurd Defense of Its Greenhouse Gas Regulations.* For an assessment of the majority opinion, see DeLong, *Supreme Climate Folly.*

FTC & Blockbuster: Oliva, *Blockbuster vs. the FTC.*

EEOC: Markay, *Feds to Trucking Company.*

Toilets/Showers/Light Bulbs: Robinson, *Fie on You Light Bulbs. Let's Talk Toilets.*

Migratory birds: American Bird Conservancy, *Oil Companies Prosecuted for Avian Deaths but Wind Companies Kill Birds with Impunity.*

AJA: R. Epstein, *Obama's Jobs Bill: Read It and Weep.*

DHS funding: Mueller & Stewart, *Terror, Security, and Money.*

Dodd-Frank & "Conflict Minerals": Zarb & Forman, *Dodd-Frank Conflict Minerals Disclosure Requirements Expected To Affect Thousands Of Public Companies In 2012.*

Durbin & debit cards: Variety of news sources.

DOJ screening of Silent Spring: PJ Tattler, *Thursday is radical movie screening day at Eric Holder's DOJ*.

Wetlands: Briefs in *Sackett v. EPA*, decided by the Supreme Court on March 21, 2012.

Civil settlements: Judicial Watch, *DOJ Steers Countrywide Settlement Cash To Leftist Groups With Dem Ties*.

Chapter Four: Diagnosis and Prognosis: Big SIS *Tomorrow*

The ratchet

Scalia: His comment was quoted in chapter 2.

Failure of reform: Rauch, *Government's End, passim*.

Supercommittee: Malkin, *K Street's Super Committee Splurge*.

The public's rational ignorance

ESA: Adler, *The Leaky Ark*.

Snail darter case: *TVA v. Hill*, 37 U.S. 153 (1978).

Shielded from ESA: Schweizer, *Throw Them All Out*, pp. xxv-xxvi.

EPA brief: Lewis, *How Absurd Is Regulating Greenhouse Gases through the Clean Air Act?*

Dodd-Frank: U.S. Chamber of Commerce, Center for Capital Markets, *Dodd-Frank Wall Street Reform and Consumer Protection Act of 2010*.

Public rallies to the wrong side: Rauch, *Government's End*, p.205.

The interests' knowledge and rapacity

"No constraint on the social cost": Olson, *Rise and Decline of Nations*, p.44.

Wetlands: See the briefs in *Sackett v. EPA*, decided by the U.S. Supreme Court on March 21, 2012.

Environmental Justice: EPA, *Environmental Justice.*
N. Dak. & birds: See chapter 2.
DOE: Sieben, *Education Dept. Issues New Guidance for Sexual-Assault Investigations.*

Noise in the system

Game show government: Arlandson, *Game Show Government.*
Sunlight Foundation: Blumenthal, *Return on Lobbying Investment: 22,000.*

Compassion traps

Compassion traps: DeLong, *The Compassion Trap.*
Penis pumps: Domenech, *Quarter-Billion Taxpayer Dollars Spent on Penis Pumps.*
Selective compassion: Dunn, *Death By Liberalism.*

Moral claims

Eric Hoffer: *Wikiquote* says the correct version, from *The Temper of Our Time*, is: "What starts out here as a mass movement ends up as a racket, a cult, or a corporation." The version given in text is the one usually quoted, and he may have said that somewhere else.
Union numbers: BLS, Union Members Summary.
EPA mercury rule: *If the Lights Go Out.* Wall Street Journal.

The Regulatory State rampant

Safeguards against faction removed: Reynolds, *Is Democracy Like Sex?* p.1653.
"Ignorant as judges": *Watts v. Indiana*, 338 U.S. 49 (1949).

Public choice: A large literature on this topic exists. A good
entry point is Simmons, *Beyond Politics*.

Takings law: DeLong, *Property Matters*.

For judicial developments during the 1970s, see DeLong,
Informal Rulemaking.

Chevron: *Chevron U.S.A. Inc. v. Natural Resources Defense
Council, Inc.*, 467 U.S. 837 (1984).

Crowded cocktail party: Personal conversation quoted by
Wald, *Some Observations on the Use of Legislative History*.

Congressional Review Act: Congressional Research
Service, *Report to Congress, Congressional Review of Agency
Rulemaking: An Update and Assessment of The Congressional
Review Act after a Decade*.

REINS: Gattuso, *Taking the REINS on Regulation*.

Clinton's regulatory strategy: The strategy is described in
more favorable terms in an article by then-Professor,
now Justice, Elena Kagan, *Presidential Administration*.

Agency incentive structures: DeLong, *New Wine*.

The Ruling Class as a special interest

Moral claims on wealth: Will, *Elizabeth Warren, and liberalism*.

Tank commander: Gavin Lyall, *Uncle Target* (1988). My use
of the example should not be taken as an insult to Major
Harry Maxim, who is a most satisfactory fictional action
hero.

Cost of law review articles: Anderson, *The Cost of a Law
Review Article*.

Dependence index: Beach & Tyrrell, *The 2010 Index of
Dependence on Government*.

Evan Thomas on the media effect: The exchange is quoted
in Groseclose, *Left Turn*, p.219. Thomas backtracked
later to say that the media was worth "maybe" five points.

Tea Party quote: Fernandez, *Storming the Castle*.

Campaign finance

Smith quotation: B. Smith, *Unfree Speech*, p.xi.

Number of PACs: *Citizens United v. FCC*, 558 U.S. __ (2010), majority slip opinion, *p.22.*

Citizens United website: www.citizensunited.org/who-we-are.aspx .

Tribal contributions: Capriccioso, *Tribes Among Biggest Campaign Contributors.*

Executive Order on disclosing contributions: OMB Watch, *Small Businesses Back Draft Executive Order Combating Pay-to-Play.*

Political legitimacy revisited

Rasmussen poll: Rasmussen Reports, *20 percent Say U.S. Government Has Consent of the Governed.*

Gallup poll: Gallup, *Americans Express Historic Negativity Toward U.S. Government.*

Gallup poll: Gallup, *Americans Most Confident in Military, Least in Congress.*

Dependence index: Beach & Tyrrell, *The 2010 Index of Dependence on Government.*

Social Security recipients: Social Security Online, *Research, Statistics, & Policy Analysis.*

Democrats' campaign strategy: The report appeared in the *New York Times* on Nov. 28, 2011, and was widely commented on.

Mandate of Heaven: See the discussion at Word IQ.

Monty Pelerin (pseudonym): The Mount Pelerin Society "is composed of persons who continue to see the dangers to civilized society...in the expansion of government, not least in state welfare, in the power of trade unions and business monopoly, and in the continuing threat and reality of inflation."

www.montpelerin.org/montpelerin/home.html
Pelerin's list: Pelerin, *Kevorkian Economics*.

Down the slippery slope

Recent Fukuyama article: Francis Fukuyama, *Friedrich A. Hayek, Big-Government Skeptic*.
Smith "a lot of ruin": This is a frequently cited quotation. See Library of Economics & Liberty: *Life of Adam Smith*.
"Whig history": For a definition, see *Word IQ*.
Ferguson quotation: Ferguson, *America's 'Oh Sh*t' Moment*.
Climate change proposals: Bailey, *Delusional in Durban*.
Electric grid: *If the Lights Go Out*. Wall Street Journal.
Population: U.S. Bureau of the Census, *Urban and Rural Populations: 1790 to 1990*.

Chapter Five: An Alternative to Big SIS: Renewing the Republic

Not a democracy, a republic

Greve quotes: Greve, *Commerce, Competition, and the Court*.

The positive use of self-interest

"If men were angels": *Federalist No. 51*.

Repeat over and over: "collective action problem"

Reynolds: *Army of Davids*.

An immediate agenda

Slaughter the sacred cows

Aug. 4: Fitzsimmons, *The Night the Old Regime Ended.*

Pressure your own special interest representative

"Current entitlement structure": Pipes, *Medicare is Increasingly a Benefit Enjoyed by The "One Percenters".*

Legal education and reform

Ninth and Tenth Amendments:
IX. The enumeration in the Constitution of certain rights shall not be construed to deny or disparage others retained by the people.
X. The powers not delegated to the United States by the Constitution, nor prohibited by it to the States, are reserved to the States respectively, or to the people.
Senators: Zywicki and Somin, *Ramifications of Repealing the 17th Amendment.*

Back to the future on nominating presidential candidates

Political parties: Cost, *Let's Go Back to the Old Nomination System.*

Coda

Rising or setting sun: Many sources.

References

References are divided into five categories:
Books;
Major Articles, Studies, and Monographs;
Government Sources;
News Clips, Weblogs, and Miscellaneous; and
Legal Decisions.

A word is needed to explain the format of the entries, which follows no known stylebook. The conventional hierarchy of putting articles and book chapters in quotation marks, journals and books in italics, and free-standing papers arbitrarily in one or the other is poorly suited to the Internet Age. Articles are available as stand-alone items from sources other than journals, many citations are to papers available on websites, a magazine may publish a blog entry or column that never sees print, and associations and non-profits classify their output in idiosyncratic ways.

Therefore, this book uses a simplified style that minimizes the number of taxonomic decisions that must be made by the author. Also, a combination of quotation marks and italic type creates typographical clutter in the e-book format. Therefore, quotation marks are not used, and the following rules apply:

For books, the references follow the spare legal style of providing only the author, title, and year, as that is all that is needed to locate them.

For shorter works, more detail is provided. The reference starts with the author, then provides the title in italics, regardless of origin or length. Source information follows, in roman, whether the source is a journal, website, or blog. Then comes the date.

Other materials, such as legal cases or websites, are patterned on these rules.

Web links are not included because everything should be easy to find via search engine. The website that supports this book will contain links, however. See www.specialintereststate.org.

Books

Adams, Jr., Charles Francis. *Railroads: Their Origin and Problems* (1878).

Anderson, Terry L. & Hill, Peter J. *The Not So Wild, Wild West: Property Rights on the Frontier* (2004).

Axelrod, Robert. *The Complexity of Cooperation: Agent-Based Models of Competition and Collaboration* (1997).

Axelrod, Robert. *The Evolution of Cooperation* (1984).

Banning, Lance. *The Jeffersonian Persuasion: Evolution of a Party Ideology* (1978).

Banning, Lance. *The Sacred Fire of Liberty: James Madison and the Founding of the Federal Republic* (1995).

Barnett, Randy E. *Restoring the Lost Constitution: The Presumption of Liberty* (2004).

Bastiat, Frederic. *The Law* (1850).

Bell, Daniel. *Beyond Liberal Democracy: Political Thinking for an East Asian Context* (2006).

Bell, Larry. *Climate of Corruption: Politics and Power Behind The Global Warming Hoax* (2011).

Bensel, Franklin. *Yankee Leviathan: The Origins of Central State Authority in America, 1859-1877* (1990, 1994).

Bensel, Franklin. *The Political Economy of American Industrialization, 1877–1900* (2000).

Bensel, Franklin. *Sectionalism and American Political Development, 1880–1980* (1987).

Bowman, James. *Media Madness: The Corruption of Our Political Culture* (2008).

Brinton, Crane. *The Anatomy of Revolution* (1939, 1956).

Browning, Edgar K. *Stealing from Each Other: How the Welfare State Robs Americans of Money and Spirit* (2008).

Brooks, Arthur. *The Battle: How the Fight Between Free Enterprise and Big Government Will Shape America's Future* (2010).

Buck, Paul. *The Road to Reunion, 1865–1900* (1938).

Burford, Anne M. *Are You Tough Enough? An Insider's View of Washington Power Politics* (1986).

Carney, Timothy B. *Obamanomics: How Barack Obama Is Bankrupting You and Enriching His Wall Street Friends, Corporate Lobbyists, and Union Bosses* (2009).

Carp, Benjamin. *Defiance of the Patriots: The Boston Tea Party & the Making of America* (2010).

Chandler, Jr., Alfred P. *The Railroads: The Nation's First Big Business* (1965).

Chandler, Jr., Alfred P. *The Visible Hand* (1977).

Clemenceau, Georges. *American Reconstruction 1865–1870* (1928).

Coburn, MD, Tom A. *Breach of Trust: How Washington Turns Outsiders into Insiders* (2003).

Crawford, Jay Boyd. *The Credit Mobilier of America: Its Origin and History* (1880).

DeLong, James V. *Out of Bounds and Out of Control: Regulatory Enforcement at the EPA* (2002).

DeLong, James V. *Property Matters: How Property Rights Are Under Assault—And Why You Should Care* (1997).

De Soto, Hernando. *The Mystery of Capital: Why Capitalism Triumphs in the West and Fails Everywhere Else* (2000).

De Soto, Hernando. *The Other Path: The Economic Answer to Terrorism* (2002).

Dunn, J. R. *Death By Liberalism: The Fatal Outcome of Well-Meaning Liberal Policies* (2011).

Edwards, Chris. *Downsizing the Federal Government* (2005).

Epstein, Richard A. *Design for Liberty: Private Property, Public Administration, and the Rule of Law* (2011).

Epstein, Richard A. *How Progressives Rewrote the Constitution* (2006).

Epstein, Richard A. *Simple Rules for a Complex World* (1995).

Epstein, Richard A. *Takings: Private Property and the Power of Eminent Domain* (1985).

Fernandez, Richard. *Storming the Castle* (2011).

Fine, Sidney. *Laissez Faire and the General Welfare State: A Study of Conflict in American Thought, 1865–1901* (1956, 1964)

Fitzgerald, Michael W. *Splendid Failure: Postwar Reconstruction in the American South* (2007).

Fitzsimmons, Michael P. *The Night the Old Regime Ended* (1998).

Flynn, John T. *The Roosevelt Myth* (1948, 1998).

Gillman, Howard. *The Constitution Besieged: The Rise & Demise of Lochner Era Police Powers Jurisprudence* (1993, 1995).

Ginger, Ray. *Altgeld's America: The Lincoln Ideal Versus Changing Realities* (1958).

Goklany, Indur M. *The Precautionary Principle: A Critical Appraisal of Environmental Risk Assessment* (2001).

Goldberg, Jonah. *Liberal Fascism: The Secret History of the American Left, From Mussolini to the Politics of Meaning* (2008).

Goodrich, Carter. *Government Promotion of American Canals and Railroads, 1800–1890* (1960).

Groseclose, Tim. *Left Turn: How Liberal Media Bias Distorts the American Mind* (2011).

Hacker, Jacob S. & Pierson, Paul. *Winner Take All Politics: How Washington Made the Rich Richer and Turned Its Back on the Middle Class* (2011).

Hamilton, Alexander; Madison, James; Jay, John. *The Federalist: A Commentary on the Constitution of the United States* (1788).

Handlin, Oscar & Handlin, Mary Flug. *Commonwealth: A Study of the Role of Government in the American Economy: Massachusetts, 1774–1861* (rev. ed.) (1947, 1969).

Harris, Lee. *The Next American Civil War: The Populist Revolt Against the Liberal Elite* (2010).

Hayek, F. A. *The Constitution of Liberty* (Vol. 17 of *The Collected Works of F. A. Hayek*, Ronald Hamowy, ed.) (1960, 2011).

Higgs, Robert. *Depression, War, and Cold War: Challenging the Myth of Conflict and Prosperity* (2006).

John, Richard R. (ed.). *Ruling Passions: Political Economy in Nineteenth-century America* (2006).

Kaiser, Robert G. *So Damn Much Money: The Triumph of Lobbying and the Corrosion of American Government* (2010).

Keller, Morton. America's *Three Regimes: A New Political History* (2007).

Kling, Arnold & Schulz, Nick. *From Poverty to Prosperity: Intangible Assets, Hidden Liabilities and the Lasting Triumph Over Scarcity* (2009).

Kolko, Gabriel. *Railroads and Regulation: 1877–1916* (1965).

Kotkin, Stephen. *Uncivil Society: 1989 and the Implosion of the Communist Establishment* (2009).

Lebedoff, David. *The Uncivil War: How a New Elite Is Destroying Our Democracy* (2004).

Lessig, Lawrence. *Republic, Lost: How Money Corrupts Congress—and a Plan to Stop It* (2011).

Livermore, Mary A. *My Story Of The War: The Civil War Memoirs Of the Famous Nurse, Relief Organizer, And Suffragette* (1888, 1995).

Lowi, Theodore. *The End of Liberalism: Ideology, Policy, and the Crisis of Public Authority* (1969).

Lucas, James W. *Timely Renewed: Amendments to Restore the American Constitution* (2010).

Maier, Pauline. *American Scripture: Making the Declaration of Independence* (1997).

Maier, Pauline. *From Resistance to Revolution: Colonial Radicals and the development of American opposition to Britain, 1765–1776* (1991).

Maier, Pauline. *Ratification: The People Debate the Constitution, 1787–1789* (2010).

Malanga, Steven. *The New New Left: How American Politics Works Today* (2005).

Manheim Jarol B. *Biz-War and the Out-of-Power Elite: The Progressive-Left Attack on the Corporation* (2004).

Mayer, David N. *Liberty of Contract: Rediscovering a Lost Constitutional Right* (2011).

McDonald, Forrest. *Novus Ordo Seclorum: The Intellectual Origins of the Constitution* (1985).

Melosi, Martin. *Garbage in the Cities: Refuse, Reform, and the Environment* (1981, 2005).

Miller, Marion Mills. *Great Debates in American History*, Vol. 11 (1915).

Moley, Raymond. *The First New Deal* (1966).

Murray, Iain. *Stealing You Blind: How Government Fat Cats Are Getting Rich Off of You* (2011).

Niskanen, William. *Reaganomics: An Insider's Account of the Policies and the People* (1988).

North, Douglass C.; Wallis, John Joseph; & Weingast, Barry R. *Violence and Social Orders: A Conceptual Framework for Interpreting Recorded Human History* (2009).

Olson, Mancur. *The Logic of Collective Action: Public Goods and the Theory of Groups* (1965).

Olson, Mancur. *Power and Prosperity: Outgrowing Communist and Capitalist Dictatorships* (2000).

Olson, Mancur. *The Rise and Decline of Nations: Economic Growth, Stagflation, and Social Rigidities* (1982).

Poundstone, William. *Prisoner's Dilemma: John von Neumann, Game Theory, and the Puzzle of the Bomb* (1992).

Powell, Jim. *FDR's Folly: How Roosevelt and His New Deal Prolonged the Great Depression* (2003).

Rahe, Paul. *Soft Despotism, Democracy's Drift: Montesquieu, Rousseau, Tocqueville, and the Modern Prospect* (2009).

Rasmussen, Scott & Schoen, Douglas. *Mad as Hell: How the Tea Party Movement Is Fundamentally Remaking Our Two-Party System* (2010).

Rauch, Jonathan. *Demosclerosis: The Silent Killer of American Government* (1994).

Rauch, Jonathan. *Government's End: Why Washington Stopped Working* (1999).

Reynolds, Glenn. *An Army of Davids: How Markets and Technology Empower Ordinary People to Beat Big Media, Big Government, and Other Goliaths* (2006).

Schelling, Thomas C. *Micromotives and Macrobehavior* (rev. ed.) (1978, 2006).

Schelling, Thomas C. *The Strategy of Conflict* (1960, 1980).

Schweizer, Peter. *Throw Them All Out: How Politicians and Their Friends Get Rich Off Insider Stock Tips, Land Deals, and Cronyism that Would Send the Rest of Us to Prison* (2011).

Shellenberger, Michael & Nordhaus, Ted. *Break Through: From the Death of Environmentalism to the Politics of Possibility* (2007).

Shlaes, Amity. *The Forgotten Man: A New History of the Great Depression* (2008).

Silverglate, Harvey. *Three Felonies a Day: How the Feds Target the Innocent* (2009, 2011).

Simmons, Randy. *Beyond Politics: The Roots of Government Failure* (rev. ed.) (2011).

Simpson, Brooks D. *The Reconstruction Presidents* (1998).

Smith, Bradley M. *Unfree Speech: The Folly of Campaign Finance Reform* (2001).

Sproat, John G. *"The Best Men": Liberal Reformers in the Gilded Age* (1968).

Tanner, Michael D. *Leviathan on the Right: How Big-Government Conservativism Brought Down the Republican Revolution* (2007).

Trzupek, Rich. *Regulators Gone Wild: How the EPA Is Ruining American Industry* (2011).

Tushnet, Mark. *The New Constitutional Order* (2003).

Usselman, Steven W. *Regulating Railroad Innovation: Business, Technology, and Politics in America, 1840–1920* (2002).

Vorenberg, Michael. *Final Freedom: The Civil War, the Abolition of Slavery, and the Thirteenth Amendment* (2001).

White, G. Edward. *The Constitution and the New Deal* (2000).

Wildavsky, Aaron. *The Politics of the Budgetary Process* (3d ed.) (1964, 1974, 1979).

Wood, Robert C. *Whatever Possessed the President? Academic Experts and Presidential Policy, 1960–1988* (1993).

Major Articles, Studies, and Monographs

Acemoglu, Daron et al. *The Consequences of Radical Reform: The French Revolution.* MIT Dept of Economics Wkg Paper No. 09-08 (2009).

Adler, Jonathan. *The Leaky Ark: The failure of endangered species protection on private land.* The American (Oct. 5, 2011).

Baker, John. *Revisiting the Explosive Growth of Federal Crimes.* Heritage Foundation (June 16, 2008).

Beach, William & Tyrrell, Patrick. *The 2010 Index of Dependence on Government.* Heritage Foundation (Oct. 14, 2010), p.25.

Bernstein, David. *Lochner and Constitutional Continuity.* Journal of Supreme Court History, Vol. 36, No. 2, pp. 116–28 (July 2011).

Bernstein, David. *Lochner, Parity, and the Chinese Laundry Cases.* 41 William & Mary Law Review 211 (1999).

Biggs, Andrew & Richwine, Jason. *Assessing the compensation of public school teachers.* American Enterprise Institute (Nov. 1, 2011).

Brinkley, Alan. *The New Deal and the Idea of the State,* in, *The Rise and Fall of the New Deal Order, 1930–1980* (Steve Fraser & Gary Gerstle, eds.) (1989).

Butler, Stephen. *Hidden Fees in 401(k) Plans.* Memorandum to U.S. House of Representatives, Committee on Education & Labor (March 6, 2007).

Clay, Henry. *In Defense of the American System.* Speech to the U.S. Senate (Feb. 2/3/6, 1832).

Codevilla, Angelo M. *America's Ruling Class—And the Perils of Revolution.* American Spectator (July/Aug 2010).

Cost, Jay. *Let's Go Back to the Old Nomination System.* Weekly Standard (Dec. 24, 2011).

Crews, Wayne. *Ten Thousand Commandments: An Annual Snapshot of the Federal Regulatory State (2011 Edition).* Competitive Enterprise Institute (April 18, 2011).

Cushman, Barry. *The Great Depression and the New Deal* (2005), for *The Cambridge History of Law in America* (Tomlins & Grossberg, eds.).

Cushman, Barry. *Mr. Dooley and Mr. Gallup: Public Opinion and Constitutional Change in the 1930s.* 50 Buffalo Law Review 7 (2002).

Cushman, Barry. *Regime Theory and Unenumerated Rights: A Cautionary Note.* 9 Journal of Constitutional Law 263 (Oct. 2006).

Cushman, Barry. *Some Varieties and Vicissitudes of Lochnerism.* 85 Boston University Law Review 101 (2005).

Dauber, Michele Landis. *The Sympathetic State.* Stanford Law School, Research Paper No. 77 (Jan. 2004).

DeLong, James V. *Avoiding a Tech Train Wreck.* The American (May/June 2008).

DeLong, James V. *The Coming of the Fourth American Republic.* The American (April 21, 2009).

DeLong, James V. *The Compassion Trap.* The American (July 29, 2011).

DeLong, James V. *The New Trustbusters.* Reason (March 1999).

DeLong, James V. *Privatizing Superfund: How to Clean Up Hazardous Waste.* Cato Institute Policy Analysis No. 247 (Dec. 18, 1995).

DeLong, James V. *Supreme Climate Folly.* The American (Dec. 18, 2009).

DeLong, James V. *The Tea Party movement and our collective interest.* Tea Party Review (April 2011).

Eastman, John C. *Restoring the 'General' to the General Welfare Clause.* 4 Chapman Law Review 63 (2001).

Edwards, Chris. *Federal Aid-to-State Programs Top 1,100.* Cato Institute Tax & Budget Bulletin No. 63 (Feb. 2011).

Epstein, Alex. *Vindicating Capitalism: The Real History of the Standard Oil Company.* MasterResource—a Free Market Energy Blog (2011).

Epstein, Richard A. *Obama's Jobs Bill: Read It and Weep.* Hoover Institution, Defining Ideas (Sept. 27, 2011).

Folsom, Burton. *John D. Rockefeller and the Oil Industry.* The Freeman (Oct 1988).

Foner, Eric. *Book Review of David W. Blight, Race and Reunion: The Civil War in American Memory.* New York Times Book Review (March 4, 2001).

Frezza, Bill. *Exactly What Is Crony Capitalism, Anyway?* Real Clear Politics (Dec. 12, 2011).

Fukuyama, Francis. *Friedrich A. Hayek, Big-Government Skeptic.* New York Times Sunday Book Review (May 06, 2011).

Gillman, Howard. *Disaster Relief, "Do Anything" Spending Powers, and the New Deal.* Law & History Review (Summer 2005), p. 443.

Gillman, Howard. *Party Politics and Constitutional Change: The Political Origins of Liberal Judicial Activism.* Digital Commons@UM Carey Law (March 2006).

Gillman, Howard. *Political Development and the Origins of the Living Constitution.* American Constitution Society for Law & Policy (Sept. 2007).

Gillman, *Howard. Regime Politics, Jurisprudential Regimes, and Unenumerated Rights.* Journal of Constitutional Law, Vol.9, p.107 (Oct. 2006).

Greenhut, Stephen. *California's Secret Government.* City Journal (Spring 2011).

Greve, Michael. *America's Upside-Down Constitution.* Address at the 2011 Transatlantic Law Forum on Constitutionalism in Crisis (Oct. 28, 2011).

Greve, Michael. *Commerce, Competition, and the Court: An Agenda for a Constitutional Revival.* American Enterprise Institute, Bradley Lecture (March 2, 2009).

Greve, Michael. *Our Defunct Commercial Constitution.* National Review (May 17, 2010).

Hanna, Autumn; Lehrer, Eli; Schreiber, Benjamin; & Slocum, Tyson. *Green Scissors: Cutting Wasteful and Environmentally Harmful Spending.* Taxpayers for Common Sense/Heartland Institute/Friends of the Earth/Public Citizen. (2011).

Henderson, David. *Of Price and Men.* Red Herring (June 1, 2000).

Higgs, Robert. *Eighteen Problematic Propositions in the Analysis of the Growth of Government.* 5 Review of Austrian Economics, Vol.5, No.1, p.3 (Jan. 1, 1991).

Horwitz, Steven. *Herbert Hoover: Father of the New Deal.* Cato Institute Briefing Paper No. 122 (Sept. 29, 2011).

Hutcheson, Matthew D. *Are Hidden Fees Undermining Employment Retirement Income Security?* Statement to U.S. House of Representatives, Comm. on Education & Labor, (March 6, 2007).

Kagan, Elena. *Presidential Administration.* 114 Harvard Law Review 2245 (2001).

Kane, Ed. *Measuring Systemic Risk to Empower the Taxpayer.* Interview, Institute for New Economic Thinking (Oct. 28, 2011).

Keating, David. *A Taxing Trend: The Rise in Complexity, Forms, and Paperwork Burdens.* National Taxpayers Union Policy Paper 127 (April 15, 2010).

Kickler, Troy. *Is Anything Free?: Debates Regarding Internal Improvements in Antebellum North Carolina.* North Carolina History Project (no date given).

King, Jr., Martin Luther. *Letter from Birmingham Jail* (April 16, 1963).

Kopel, David B. *How the British Gun Control Program Precipitated the American Revolution.* Social Sciences Research Network (SSRN) (Dec. 9, 2011) (forthcoming in Charleston Law Review).

Laffer, Arthur. *The Economic Burden Caused by Tax Code Complexity.* Laffer Center (April 14, 2011).

Lewis, Alfred Henry. *The People or the Railroads?* Hearst Magazine, pp. 506–520 (Oct. 1913).

Lincoln, Abraham. *Second Lecture on Discoveries and Inventions.* Jacksonville, IL (Feb. 11, 1859).

Mahoney, Paul. *The Political Economy of the Securities Act of 1933.* Univ. of Virginia School of Law, Law & Economics Wkg Paper No. 00-11 (May 2000).

Malysheva, Nadezhda & Walter, John R. *How Large Has the Federal Safety Net Become?* Richmond Federal Reserve Bank, Wkg Paper No. 10-03 (May 2010).

Missouri-Kansas City Law School: *Lynching in America: Statistics, Information, Images* (no date given).

PJ Media. *Every Single One.* (Aug. 08–Sept. 26, 2011) (12-part series by various authors).

Ranney, Joseph. *The Making of the Wisconsin Constitution.* Wisconsin Lawyer (10-part series, published in book form as *Trusting Nothing to Providence: History of Wisconsin's Legal System* (2000).)

Paine, Thomas. *Common Sense* (1776).

Pilon, Roger. *The United States Constitution: From Limited Government to Leviathan.* American Institute for Economic Research, Economic Education Bulletin, Vol. XLV, No. 12 (December 2005).

Powell, Jim. *Obama And Teddy Roosevelt: Both Progressives, Both Clueless About The Economy.* Forbes (Dec. 8, 2011).

Reynolds, Glenn. *Is Democracy Like Sex?* 48 Vanderbilt Law Review 1635 (1995).

Ripley, William Z. *Railroad Construction Finance in America: A Comprehensive, Unbiased Study of the Methods that Have Been Used to Raise Money for American Railroads.* Railway Age Gazette, Vol. 56, Nos. 22 & 23 (1914).

Roosevelt, Franklin Delano. *Address at Oglethorpe University.* New Deal Network, Works of Franklin D. Roosevelt (May 22, 1932).

Scalia, Antonin. *Considering the Role of Judges Under the Constitution of the United States.* Testimony to the Senate Judiciary Committee (Oct. 5, 2011).

Schizer, David. *Fiscal Policy in an Era of Austerity.* Columbia Law and Economics Wkg Paper No. 408 (Oct. 17. 2011).

Sunstein, Cass R. *Naked Preferences and the Constitution.* 84 Columbia Law Review 1689 (1984).

Thies, Clifford. *The American Railroad Network during the Early 19th Century: Private versus Public Enterprise.* Cato Journal, Vol. 22, No. 2 (Fall 2002).

Wald, Patricia M. *Some Observations on the Use of Legislative History in the 1981 Supreme Court Term,* 68 Iowa Law Review 195 (1982).

Wallis, John Joseph. *The Concept of Systemic Corruption in American History,* in *Corruption and Reform: Lessons from America's Economic History* (Glaeser & Goldin, eds.) (2006).

Wallis, John Joseph. *Constitutions, Corporations, and Corruption: American States and Constitutional Change, 1842–1852.* National Bureau of Economic Research Wkg Paper No. 10451 (April 2004).

Walter, John R. & Weinberg, Walter. *How Large is the Federal Financial Safety Net?* Cato Journal, Vol. 21, No. 3, p.369 (Winter 2002).

Williams, Ryan C. *The One and Only Substantive Due Process Clause.* 120 Yale Law Journal 408 (2010).

Williams, Stephen F. *Transitions Into—And Out Of—Liberal Democracy.* The Fifth Annual Friedrich A. von Hayek

Lecture: New York Univ. Journal of Law & Liberty, Vol. 5, p.245 (2010).

Yandle, Bruce. *Bootleggers and Baptists: The Education of a Regulatory Economist.* Regulation, Vol. 7, No. 3 (1983).

Yandle, Bruce. *Bootleggers and Baptists in Retrospect.* Regulation, Vol. 22. No. 3 (1998).

Zywicki, Todd & Somin, Ilya. *Ramifications of Repealing the 17th Amendment.* Federalist Society, Engage, Vol. 12, No. 2 (Sept. 2011).

Government Sources

Bureau of the Census. *Urban and Rural Populations: 1790 to 1990.*

Bureau of Labor Statistics. *Union Members Summary* (Jan. 21, 2011).

Congress, Joint Committee on Taxation. *Background Information on Tax Expenditure Analysis*, JCX-15-11 (March 9, 2011).

Congressional Research Service. *Report to Congress: Congressional Review of Agency Rulemaking: An Update and Assessment of The Congressional Review Act after a Decade* (May 8, 2008).

Environmental Protection Agency. *Environmental Justice.*

General Services Administration. *Catalogue of Federal Domestic Assistance.*

Government Printing Office. *Government Manual*, App. C.

National Taxpayer Advocate. *2010 Annual Report To Congress.*

Office of Management & Budget. *Analytical Perspectives, Budget of the Unites States Government, Fiscal Year 2012*, Ch. 17.

Social Security Online. *Research, Statistics, & Policy Analysis.* (Oct. 2011).

USA.gov (The U.S. government's official website portal).

News Clips, Weblogs, and Miscellaneous

American Bird Conservancy. *Oil Companies Prosecuted for Avian Deaths but Wind Companies Kill Birds With Impunity.* Media Release (Sept. 07, 2011).

American Enterprise Institute. *Is Sarbanes-Oxley Impairing Corporate Risk-Taking?* Event (June 18, 2007).

Anderson, Kenneth. *The Cost of a Law Review Article?* Blog post, The Volokh Conspiracy (April 22, 2011).

Antos, Joseph. *Still No Good News for ObamaCare.* The American (Sept. 23, 2010).

Arlandson, James. *Game Show Government.* American Thinker (Nov. 30, 2011).

Bailey, Ron. *Delusional in Durban.* Reason (Dec. 5, 2011).

Blumenthal, Paul. *Return on Lobbying Investment: 22,000%.* Sunlight Foundation (April 9, 2009).

Brown, Joshua. *Dear Jamie Dimon.* the reformed Broker (Dec. 20, 2011).

Chantrill, Christopher. *US Government Spending.* www.usgovernmentspending.com/

Chantrill, Christopher. *U.S. Government Taxes and Revenue Since 1900.* www.usgovernmentrevenue.com/revenue_history

Capriccioso, Rob. *Tribes Among Biggest Campaign Contributors.* Indian Country Today (March 22, 2011).

Cauchon, Dennis. *Student loans outstanding will Exceed $1 trillion this year.* USA Today (Oct. 25, 2011).

DeMint, Jim. *Venture socialism.* Washington Times (Sept. 27, 2011).

DeMint, Jim. *We're Still Not Cutting.* National Review (Nov. 8, 2011).

Domenech, Benjamin. *Quarter-Billion Taxpayer Dollars Spent on Penis Pumps.* Heartlander (Dec. 6, 2011).

Environmental Working Group. *2011 Farm Subsidy Data Base.*

Ferguson, Niall. *America's "Oh Sh*t" Moment.* Newsweek (Oct. 30, 2011).

Fierce Reason. *California's Unsustainable Existence, by Larry.* Blog post (Aug. 10, 2011).

Furchtgott-Roth, Diana. *Obama's Green-Energy Jobs Lie.* Real Clear Markets (Nov. 03, 2011).

Gallup. *Americans Express Historic Negativity Toward U.S. Government.* Gallup website (Sept. 26, 2011).

Gallup. *Americans Most Confident in Military, Least in Congress.* Gallup website (June 23, 2011).

Gattuso, James. *Taking the REINS on Regulation.* Heritage Foundation (Oct. 13, 2011).

Goldman, David (a.k.a. "Spengler"). *Republicans, Democrats and Wall Street Fraud or: Who's the MF Now?* PJ Media (Nov. 18, 2011).

Goldman, David (a.k.a. "Spengler"). *What do we want from Wall Street?* Asia Times (Nov. 08, 2011).

Greenhut, Stephen. *Rural rebellion brewing.* Orange County Register (Oct. 30, 2011).

Grimes, William. *Samuel H. Beer, Authority on British Government, Dies at 97.* New York Times (April 18, 2009).

Grunwald, Michael. *Why the U.S. Is Also Giving Brazilians Farm Subsidies.* Time (April 9, 2010).

Grunwald, Michael. *The Farm Bill Stalls—for Now.* Time (Nov. 17, 2007).

Hinderaker, John. *The Purpose of Government.* Blog post, Powerline (April 28, 2011).

Jacoby, Jeff. *Clunker Q & A.* Boston Globe (Aug. 26, 2009).

Judicial Watch. *DOJ Steers Countrywide Settlement Cash To Leftist Groups With Dem Ties.* Blog Post (Jan. 5, 2012).

Kocieniewski, David. *Rich Tax Breaks Bolster Makers of Video Games.* New York Times (Sept. 11, 2011).

LaFramboise, Donna. *When the Police Knock on Your Door.* Blog Post, No Frakking Consensus (Dec. 21, 2011).

Lavelle, Marianne & Lewis, Matthew. *Climate lobbying dominated by 10 firms.* Politico (May 20, 2009).

Lewis, Marlo. *How Absurd Is Regulating Greenhouse Gases through the Clean Air Act?* Blog post, GlobalWarming.org (Sept. 27, 2011).

Malkin, Michelle. *K Street's Super Committee Splurge.* Real Clear Politics (Nov. 11, 2011).

Manhattan Institute. *Trial Lawyers Inc.: Attorneys General, A Report On The Alliance Between State AGs And The Plaintiffs' Bar 2011.* Center for Legal Policy, Manhattan Institute for Public Policy Research.

Markay, Lachlan. *Feds to Trucking Company: You Cannot Fire Alcoholic Drivers.* Blog Post, Heritage Foundation (Aug. 30, 2011).

McArdle, Megan. *'Historic' Preservation.* Blog post, The Atlantic, (Aug. 8, 2011).

McElroy, David. *"I'm just quitting": A scene right out of 'Atlas Shrugged' in Birmingham.* Blog post, David McElroy (July 20, 2011).

Mueller, John & Stewart, Mark. *Terror, Security, and Money: Balancing the Risks, Benefits, and Costs of Homeland Security.* Panel presentation at the Annual Convention of the Midwest Political Science Association (April 1, 2011).

Oliva, S. M. *Blockbuster vs. the FTC (Keeping Future Competition Safe?).* Blog Post, Information Liberation (June 30, 2010).

OMB Watch. *Small Businesses Back Draft Executive Order Combating Pay-to-Play.* (May 12, 2011).

Orzag, Peter. *As Kaldor's Facts Fall, Occupy Wall Street Rises.* Bloomberg View (Oct. 18, 2011).

Pelerin, Monty. *Kevorkian Economics—Hospice Care For The Economy.* Blog post, Economic Noise (Aug 24, 2011).

Pipes, Sally. *Medicare is Increasingly a Benefit Enjoyed by The "One Percenters".* Forbes (Dec 5, 2011).

PJ Media. *Thursday is radical movie screening day at Eric Holder's DOJ.* PJ Tattler (Oct. 26, 2011).

Rasmussen. *20 percent Say U.S. Government Has Consent of the Governed.* Rasmussen Reports (Nov. 3, 2011).

Robinson, Peter. *Fie on You Light Bulbs. Let's Talk Toilets.* Ricochet (Dec. 1, 2010).

Sieben, Lauren. *Education Dept. Issues New Guidance for Sexual-Assault Investigations.* Chronicle of Higher Education (April 4, 2011).

Simmons, Daniel. *EPA's Absurd Defense of Its Greenhouse Gas Regulations.* Blog Post, Institute for Energy Research (Sept. 23. 2011).

Taxpayers for Common Sense. *Earmarks.*

Tigerhawk. *Occupy this: President Obama's Wall Street fundraising.* Blog post, Tigerhawk, (Oct. 20, 2011).

U.S. Chamber of Commerce, Center for Capital Markets, *Dodd-Frank Wall Street Reform and Consumer Protection Act of 2010: Regulatory Authority* (2011).

Wall Street Journal. *If the Lights Go Out.* Editorial. (Dec. 06, 2011).

Will, George. *Elizabeth Warren and Liberalism: Twisting the 'social contract'.* Washington Post (Oct. 5, 2011).

Zarb, Frank & Forman, Daniel. *Dodd-Frank Conflict Minerals Disclosure Requirements Expected To Affect Thousands Of Public Companies In 2012.* Metropolitan Counsel (Oct. 2011).

Legal Decisions

216 Jamaica Ave LLC v. Playhouse Realty Co., U.S. Court of Appeals for the Sixth Circuit (Aug 2008).

Antoninetti v. Chipotle Mexican Grill, U.S. Court of Appeals for the Ninth Circuit (July 2010).

Chevron U.S.A. Inc. v. Natural Resources Defense Council, Inc., 467 U.S. 837 (1984).

Citizens United v. FCC, 558 U.S. __ (2010).

Kelly v. Pittsburgh, 104 U.S. 78 (1881).

Kelo v. City of New London, 545 U.S. 469 (2005).

Sackett v. EPA. Decided by the U.S. Supreme Court on March 21, 2012. Briefs are available at: www.americanbar. org/publications/preview_home/10-1062.html.

Silveira v Lockyer, 312 F.3d 1052 (9th Cir. 2002). Judge Kozinski's statement on the Second Amendment is in his 2003 dissent from the Order Denying Petition for Rehearing En Banc. The dissent is hard to locate in the normal public domain legal databases, but it can be found at: http://archive.ca9.uscourts.gov/ca9/newopinions.nsf /019661EF3BAAF4C488256D1D00793D3A/$file/011509 8o.pdf?openelement.

Slaughter-House Cases, 83 U.S. 36 (1873).

TVA v. Hill, 437 U.S. 153 (1978).

U.S. v. Carolene Products, 304 U.S. 144 (1938).

U.S. v. Cruikshank, 92 U.S. 542 (1875).

Watts v. Indiana, 338 U.S. 49 (1949).

Wickard v. Filburn, 317 U.S. 111 (1942).

Acknowledgments

An author requires the help of many people, even if many are unaware at the time that they are contributing. My circle of gratitude is wide.

It starts with my colleagues back in the old U.S. Bureau of the Budget in the 1960s, especially Paul Feldman, who first got me to doubt the progressive pieties I brought with me from Harvard. I should also thank the top management of the federal agencies for which I worked for their contributions to demonstrating so vividly why Paul's skepticism of government was, if anything, understated.

Later, colleagues at the Federal Trade Commission and the Administrative Conference of the United States were valuable teachers, particularly the late Jim Liebeler and Philip Harter. Over the years, I have also profited greatly from many smart and dedicated friends in the world of free-market think tanks. Included are Fred Smith, Wayne Crews, James Gattuso, and the whole gang at CEI; Ray Gifford, Garland McCoy, Adam Thierer, and Solveig Singleton at

PFF; Jerry Taylor, Roger Pilon, and the late Bill Niskannen at Cato; Nick Schulz and Michael Greve at AEI; the editors of *Reason*, starting with Virginia Postrel; and Jon Henke and the others at Digital Society.

I also enjoyed my time as a consultant, particularly when I worked with Martha Beauchamp, Steve Swanson, Walter Gawlak, William O'Keefe, Charles DiBona, Elizabeth Treanor, Sully Curran, and others at the American Petroleum Institute during the 1980s and 1990s—they showed how good trade association staff, willing and determined to deal honestly with public issues, can make significant contributions to the general welfare.

My family, including Christopher L. DeLong, Julia D. Mahoney, J. Bradford DeLong, Paul Mahoney, and Dianne Wyss, is a continuous source of information, challenge, and help. Particular thanks go to Julia for comments on this essay and to Dianne for demonstrating the indomitable nature of American entrepreneurial determination.

And, of course, the Tea Parties and all citizen activists have triggered a sense of optimism that reform is possible and that the American spirit will rise to the demands of the age and renew the Republic. We owe them a huge debt.

Homage is also due the authors listed in the References, particularly Mancur Olson and other writers on collective action issues, such as Thomas Schelling, William Poundstone, and Jonathan Rauch, who coined "demosclerosis" more than fifteen years ago. Add the scholars who are invigorating our understanding of American history to provide clearer views of both the nineteenth century and the New Deal. The list is too long to exhaust, but I have relied mainly on the work of Richard Epstein, Robert Higgs, Barry Cushman, Howard Gillman, David Bernstein, Amity Shlaes, John Chapman, Michael Greve, Randy Burnett, and Jim Powell.

The Internet and the blogosphere have made projects such as this one possible in a way that was simply not the case a few years ago. The firehose of information, links, anecdotes, and analyses puts so much information at one's door so quickly that one has the luxury of reviewing and considering an enormous amount of information rather than spending all day trying to dig out one fact at a time.

So thank you Powerline, Social Sciences Research Network, PJ Media, the American, AmericanThinker, Commentary, the American Interest, the RealClear family, Right Coast, Ricochet, Hot Air, Dr. Sanity, Instapundit, RedState, HumanEvents, Manhattan ~Institute, Reason's Hit-and-Run, Heartland, CEI, Cato, Aleph, Drudge, Megan McArdle, the Breitbart Big collection, Café Hayek, EconoLog, and .... and .... through a long list.

And finally, my anonymous copy editor at Create Space did an excellent job of preventing mistakes and forcing me to clarify ambiguities. She is not to blame for my insistence on using an idiosyncratic style for references that is designed to minimize my own inconvenience, or for the errors that crept back in during re-editing.

About the Author

James V. DeLong has lived in Washington, DC, for four decades. He has been a lawyer, middle-manager, analyst, and research director for federal agencies; an executive and writer at market-oriented think tanks; a foundation executive; and a free-lance lawyer/consultant.

His substantive experience encompasses energy and the environment; administrative law and procedure; property rights; intellectual property; and high tech/telecom.

The list of his employers includes the Department of Housing and Urban Development; the Bureau of the Budget; the Federal Trade Commission; the Administrative Conference of the United States; the Drug Abuse Council; the National Legal Center for the Public Interest; the Competitive Enterprise Institute; the Progress & Freedom Foundation; the Digital Society; and the Convergence Law Institute. He is an Adjunct Scholar of CEI and a member of the Board of Advisors of the Heartland Institute.

Mr. DeLong is the author of two books: *Property Matters: How Property Rights Are Under Assault—And Why You Should Care* (Free Press 1997) and *Out of Bounds and Out of Control: Regulatory Enforcement at the EPA* (Cato Institute 2002). He has also written numerous white papers and blogs for his think-tank employers and articles for *The American, National Review, Claremont Review of Books, Tea Party Review,* and *Reason.*

A bibliography is at the website for this book, www.specialintereststate.org.

He is a *cum laude* graduate of Harvard College, where he majored in American History, and a *magna cum laude* graduate of the Harvard Law School, where he served as Book Review Editor of the *Law Review.*

Made in the USA
Lexington, KY
17 June 2012